Live Long & Strong!

Dr. Steve

Proverbs 11:25

CELEBRATE 100

CENTENARIAN SECRETS to SUCCESS in BUSINESS and LIFE

CELEBRATE

100

CENTENARIAN SECRETS *to* SUCCESS *in* BUSINESS *and* LIFE

STEVE FRANKLIN, PH.D., *and* **LYNN PETERS ADLER**, J.D.

WILEY

Cover Design: Wiley
Cover Image: © iStockphoto.com/mammuth

Published by John Wiley & Sons, Inc., Hoboken, New Jersey.
Published simultaneously in Canada.

For general information on our other products and services or for technical support, please contact our Customer Care Department within the United States at (800) 762-2974, outside the United States at (317) 572-3993 or fax (317) 572-4002.

Wiley publishes in a variety of print and electronic formats and by print-on-demand. Some material included with standard print versions of this book may not be included in e-books or in print-on-demand. If this book refers to media such as a CD or DVD that is not included in the version you purchased, you may download this material at http://booksupport.wiley.com. For more information about Wiley products, visit www.wiley.com.

Library of Congress Cataloging-in-Publication Data:

Franklin, Steve, 1947-
    Celebrate 100 : centenarian secrets to success in business and life/Steve Franklin and Lynn Peters Adler.
    pages cm
      Includes bibliographical references.
    ISBN 978-1-118-52564-7 (cloth)—ISBN 978-1-118-56774-6—ISBN 978-1-118-56755-5—ISBN 978-1-118-56762-3
      1. Centenarians. 2. Longevity. 3. Success. 4. Success in business.
  I. Adler, Lynn Peters, 1943- II. Title. III. Title: Celebrate one hundred.
  HQ1061.F657 2013
  650.1—dc23
                                    2013006163

Printed in the United States of America

10 9 8 7 6 5 4 3 2 1

To all the gracious, generous Centenarians and their lovely families who shared precious time and priceless wisdom with us for the benefit of current and future generations.

CONTENTS

CHAPTER 3   75

MONEY WISE AND TIME TESTED

CHAPTER 4   101

WORK WISDOM

FOREWORD

I am a centenarian wannabe.

Reaching 100 is a great life goal because I have heard that not many people die over 100!

My good friend Steve Franklin and his colleague Lynn Adler have written books, articles, and given speeches all over the world, and *Celebrate 100: Centenarian Secrets for Success in Business and Life* is their best work ever.

Their combined videotaping, interviewing, and surveying of over 500 centenarians to capture their wisdom and advice about money, work, and life is a wonderful accomplishment. Working hard to share their priceless "secrets" and wisdom with the younger generation through this book is a great contribution to our society.

The English writer Samuel Johnson said that most people don't need to be taught anything new—they just need to be reminded to do what they already know they should be doing.

For some of you, the wisdom and advice presented in *Celebrate 100* will teach you some "new" ideas that I hope you will put into practice if you want to live a long and prosperous life. For the rest of you, *Celebrate 100* will be an enjoyable "reminder" of what you already know you should be doing to live a full and productive life, no matter how long you live.

I hope you will embrace and practice the centenarian secrets about money, work, and life as you enjoy their interesting stories, witty comments, and observations from over a century of dynamic change and living life to the fullest.

As Steve and Lynn suggest, listen to them, learn from them, and laugh with them.

If you do, you just might make it into the Centenarian Club, too.

I'm planning on it!

S. TRUETT CATHY
Founder and Chairman
Chick-fil-A, Inc.

INTRODUCTION

Century-Old Questions . . . Century-Old Answers

*"You can do anything you want if you just put
your mind on it and start working."*

BESSE COOPER, 116, FORMER SCHOOL TEACHER

Many answers to the challenging questions of life today are found in the wisdom of those who have traveled this road before us. We seek answers to our troubling economy, answers to an uncertain future, and answers that will lead to financial security, emotional stability, meaningful relationships, enjoyable work, and living life longer, healthier, and "larger." What if the answers, the secrets, to many of these challenges about money, work, and life could be found in the authentic wisdom and experiences from the past and present in America's centenarians? And, what if we fail to capture that wisdom and experience—those secrets—and share them with the younger generation? We set out to find these answers by interviewing America's oldest generation.

ABOUT *CELEBRATE 100*

Celebrate 100 is the distilled essence of over 5000 combined years of wisdom, wit, insight, perspective, and advice about life from over 500 centenarians who have lived it with determination, resolve, and excellence.

They come from all across our great nation and represent the many different cultures of our rich heritage, and they comprise all of our diverse socioeconomic strata.

They live in the country, the suburbs, and the cities. They have worked on farms and in factories, warehouses, offices, and in their homes. They have worked in government and in the private sector. They have been employees, bosses, and entrepreneurs. They have been married and divorced. They have laughed and cried—a lot. They have seen babies born and loved ones die. They are athletic and not so athletic. They are compliant and they are mavericks. They are conservative and they are liberal. They are religious and not so religious. They have served in the military and they have supported our troops. They have lived through the Roaring Twenties, the Great Depression, World Wars I and II, Elvis, the Beatles, the Internet, Cable News, space travel, and our current economic, social, and political challenges. They are givers—not takers.

They are witty and they are wise.

We traveled across America meeting with these special people whose ages ranged from 100 to over 116. We captured their goldmine of wisdom and advice through over 250 hours of videotaped interviews, extensive written questionnaires, and telephone interviews. They were born in 30 different states and in 13 foreign countries, creating a kaleidoscope of background, dialogue, and history. Many were themselves first-generation Americans.

Our centenarians were asked questions about money, work, and many aspects of life that confront every one of us. We asked them to share their wisdom, advice, and secrets about these issues from two perspectives: what they actually did that worked, or what would they recommend for the younger generation after a century of perspective, trial and error, successes and failures.

Since beginning this research endeavor in 2007 some of our centenarians have passed on to their next "chapter" in life as *Celebrate 100* goes to press. However, we write and refer to all of them in the present tense since they still are very much present in our hearts, and to represent their most recent age since our last interview, conversation, correspondence, or communication about them.

Showing up with cameras and a few inquisitive questions, we witnessed them become alive as artists who begin creatively painting a picturesque scene, musicians passionately playing their instruments, dancers gracefully flowing with their favorite movements, writers thoughtfully articulating well-spoken words, or athletes pressing toward their goal with zest and determination. They light up as they reflect on memories, as they remember and put the pieces of life together in words we, the younger generation, are blessed and privileged to hear. Perhaps the gift of time we received from them, and gave to them, during the interviews, is the best kind of gift—a gift that encouraged wisdom to be shared that leads to a more hopeful future for us all.

OUR PROMISE TO YOU

If you will dig deep into this goldmine and treasury of experiences, stories, anecdotes, poems, and prose, extract the nuggets of time-tested wise advice from each page, and daily deposit them into your personal lifestyle bank account, you will be richer, wiser, more joyful, more enthusiastic about life, and dramatically increase your personal chances for celebrating 100 years of life lived with gusto.

Listen to them. Laugh with them. Learn from them.

And you will live life—and you will love life—longer.

ACKNOWLEDGMENTS

A project like this would probably take 100 years to complete if not for many devoted team members contributing generous time and talent throughout this journey to *Celebrate 100.* Each one of you has helped with your unique gifts to make this much more than just a great book. It is an awakening and awareness and celebration of life for everyone who seeks to live long and live well. We hope every one of you experience and celebrate the centenarian spirit each day of your journey into the exciting future.

Thank you with all of our hearts.

My wonderful wife, Elaine, for your tireless data tabulating and rich content contributions; all my beautiful children and grandchildren; Leo Wells for your enthusiastic support and encouragement; centenarian research team wannabes Nancy Daniel, Kendra Emigh, Doug Buce, Joe Colavito; Andy Stanley and Jeff Henderson for your encouragement and counsel on sharpening my 100 presentations; the awesome Northpoint and Buckhead Church replenishers for your priceless feedback; Tripp Crosby, Matt Garret, and team for creative context; Debbie Woodall for design ideas; all the Cathy family for your years of amazing generosity and support; Bill Heavener, Greg Suess, and Cynthia Manson for connecting us to create this book; and my two lifetime spiritual and barbeque buddies Robert Wynne (Joker 2) and Bob Day (Joker 3). You're the best!

STEVE

(*continued*)

ACKNOWLEDGMENTS

My husband, Jim Adler, for his editorial wordsmithing and good counsel; my friend, Neil Holland, for his extraordinary dedication and collaboration, invaluable suggestions, proofreading, and contributions in research; Donald Downes for his loyalty over many years, creating and maintaining the centenarian web site and blog; Ole Amundsen for his continued interest; Rebecca Strang for lending a helping hand; and the volunteers in Phoenix who worked on survey mailings, and the 319 Venti Sea-Salt Caramel Mocha coffees from Starbucks.

I also wish to acknowledge with sincere thanks the innumerable centenarians and their families over the years for their warm response to my efforts bringing and keeping centenarians "front and center." And my twin brothers Brian and Marty Peters for their ever-present support, and posthumously, my mother, Evelyn R. Peters, who was always my steadfast advocate and best volunteer.

Lynn

CHAPTER 1

Today's Centenarians—Celebrities and National Treasures

A Century of Wisdom

THE CELEBRITIES OF AGING: CENTENARIANS IN THE SPOTLIGHT

THE AGE OF CENTENARIANS: A MILLION OR MORE BY 2050?

THE WISDOM OF CENTENARIANS: AUTHENTIC—EXPERIENCE, NOT THEORY

NATIONAL TREASURES: UNIQUE—INDIVIDUALLY AND COLLECTIVELY

CAMEOS OF TODAY'S CENTENARIANS

A CENTURY OF PROGRESS: THEIR CENTURY

People who have lived 100 years or more are here to share their experiences, having done and seen it all. They are also our living links to history and our role models for the future of aging. Their engaging spirit can help to shape the attitude of younger generations, especially Baby Boomers, who are looking toward their future years.

———— ✄◦◯◦◦ ————

"My golden years are like sparkling diamonds,"
says Elsa Brehm Hoffmann, 104.

To celebrate her 100th birthday, Elsa bought a brand new car, "eggplant color, because it was a little different." After giving herself a birthday gala for 150 friends and family, she took off on a two-week Caribbean cruise. On board she met another centenarian, John Donnelly, and his wife, Marian, who were celebrating their seventh wedding anniversary and his 102nd birthday. Meanwhile, Jack Borden, 101, was hard at work at his law firm in Texas, still handling a full caseload and loving every minute of it.

Centenarians are shattering the long-held stereotypes of life in later years, which is thought to be static, boring, and marked by disinterest in contemporary life. Today, we see active centenarians enjoying interests that are associated with much younger people, prompting us to think better of our future—30, 50, or 70 years from now. As with Elsa, John, and Jack, much of what we see in centenarians' lives is surprising—for instance, the increasing number of people who are living independently at 100 and over, and the number of centenarians still driving competently. We see centenarians living full lives: dancing, falling in love, traveling, playing in a band, taking courses, giving lectures; using cell phones, computers for e-mail, browsing the Web, socializing on Facebook and Twitter; working, volunteering, and lunching with friends. We like what we see, but how do we get there, and what "secrets" do we need to know?

The centenarians with whom you are about to become acquainted share an indomitable spirit. They tell us what has worked for them to live successfully into advanced age and they share their "secrets" of business and life. Indeed, centenarians are the true experts on living long and living well, and on what it takes to do so. Others can study them and turn them into statistics, but only they know what it is like and what it means to live for 100 years; only they can vivify the experience of reaching the century mark and beyond. Centenarians are here to share their hard-earned wisdom born of their experiences, and show us why it is worth the effort to strive to have the means to live a good life in old age.

"Think of it as mountain climbing," explains Dr. Will Clark, 104, as he sits holding the hand of his wife, Lois. "Why do people climb mountains? Because they're there. Because they can. Some people will be lost along the way, and it's never going to be easy; but for those who reach the top, there's no better view. So why give up on life? Why sell yourself short? There's so much you can learn and do and enjoy. Life can be very fulfilling if you make it so. But you've got to want to do it."

Centenarians such as Dr. and Mrs. Clark exemplify the positive attitude and other characteristics active centenarians have in common, the traits that have helped them to reach the century mark and enjoy a good quality of life at 100 and beyond. Lois, 101, says, "It's not just how long you live that matters, but how well. People forget that, I think."

"People ask all the time about how to live to 100," Dr. Clark adds. "I tell them it's easy: all you have to do is survive your 70s, 80s, and 90s, and that's the hard part!"

This "Centenarian Spirit" will become familiar to you as you learn of the lives and lifestyles of the Clarks, Elsa, John, Jack, and many others in the following pages. You will see it in action: A love of life, which includes a sense of humor and a healthy dose of self-esteem; a positive yet realistic attitude; a strong religious or spiritual belief;

personal courage, because a lot of things can go wrong as we get older, such as those that require medical intervention. And, most important, a remarkable ability to renegotiate life at every turn—to compensate—to accept the losses and changes that come with aging and not let it stop them.

"Keep good, keep busy, keep thinking about tomorrow,"
advises Carl Azar, 100.

Carl's thought could be the centenarian motto.

THE CELEBRITIES OF AGING: CENTENARIANS IN THE SPOTLIGHT

Centenarians are the celebrities of aging. They draw the most attention and capture the spotlight; they are the trendsetters. Centenarians are influencing society in ways once not imaginable. Longevity itself is one of the greatest developments of the twentieth century. Now, well into the twenty-first, growing numbers of elders are going far beyond the once touted ideal of "aging gracefully" to a new standard of "aging excellently!" And Baby Boomers are eyeing this with glee. Today's centenarians are changing the very thought of what's possible in our later years.

"It was once standard journalism for local papers to report on the event of a person in the community who had reached the remarkable age of 100, giving a chronological biography of the person's life, often mentioning the person's close family members," says Mildred Heath, 101, a longtime newspaper reporter. "It was standard fare. Nothing unusual, just what the person used to do. Today, there is more interesting copy because people who have lived to 100 and beyond are very often continuing to do things and to be involved with their communities, clubs, churches, and families. In the old days, a local resident who took a trip out of town for vacation or to visit relatives was noteworthy, and a little article made the weekly paper. Today, centenarians are among those traveling to visit family and often just for pleasure. It's really quite an extraordinary difference."

Centenarians are sought out now because of their active lifestyles, not only for print media but also television features and specials, often centering around longevity. In the spring of 2008, for example, the ABC Barbara Walters Special, "Living to 150—Can You Do It?" aired on network television. In one segment, it featured five centenarians, four of whom are included in *Celebrate 100:* Elsa Hoffmann; Lillian Cox; Karl Hartzell, PhD; and Rosie Ross. The fifth centenarian, Dorothy Young, was a performer who lived in New Jersey, and was the last living assistant to the magician Harry Houdini. The others traveled from their homes in Florida and Arizona to New York to be interviewed by Ms. Walters, who mentioned the Special in her book, *Audition,* as being one of her favorites in her long career. She related especially to Lillian Cox, she said, because of Lillian's resilience.

After the taping, the group traveled by limousine to (then) Tavern on the Green, their choice, for carriage rides through Central Park and a lovely dinner. "The after-party was almost as exciting as the main event," Elsa observed. "But it was a thrill to be interviewed by Ms. Walters, and to be on national television. A few weeks later, a film crew attended my birthday gala and footage was included."

In December of the following year, Ruth Proskauer Smith, 102, and Captain Jose Grant, 101, appeared on a network TV special, "GO! New York." Ruth, a native New Yorker, was featured because of her active lifestyle and civic involvement in her later years. For two decades she has led a weekly seminar at the City College of New York about the Supreme Court for a group of retired professionals. As an intrepid New Yorker, she travels from her home at the Dakota by subway each week. Ruth's father was a prominent New York judge and lawyer, and confidant and speechwriter of Alfred E. Smith, four-time governor of New York and unsuccessful candidate for president. Governor Smith gave Ruth her first lesson in public speaking, when, while a student at Radcliffe College, she was called upon at the last minute to introduce him at a large political event. "I was so nervous," she says, "and I didn't want to do it. But he assured me to speak my mind and I would do fine. So I did, and have been doing it—successfully—ever since."

Centenarians with Lynn in New York

Joseph "Jose" Grant was included because of his continuing role in aviation and the jewelry business he founded in Stamford, Connecticut, after retiring as a Captain from TWA. He started flying as a barnstormer in the 20s and went on to become the private pilot for the King of Saudi Arabia in the 40s, and then joined TWA. He still frequently pilots his son's private plane. Captain Grant returned to Saudi Arabia at the age of 99 and again at 101, to renew his acquaintance with the Saudi Royal Family; he helped to found their national airline in the late 40s. Recently, at 101, during the Oshkosh Air Show, actor Harrison Ford remarked "Jose was more like Indiana Jones than I was." Jose's advice to viewers of the show was: "Enjoy your life!"

Fitness magazine (Spring 2011) included four centenarians in an article encouraging healthy diet and exercise as a way to age well. Beatrice McLellan, 100, was disappointed she was not included, despite "pumping iron." New Yorker Ruth Korbin, 101, was featured in an article in the November 2012 issue of *Pilates Style* magazine as possibly the oldest Pilates student at 101. Ruth looks beautiful and stylish in the two-page spread. She began Pilates when she was 85.

Dr. Frank Shearer, 101, of Washington state, a retired family physician, made the cover of *National Geographic* and a host of other print media because of his continued passion for water skiing and horseback riding (he was shown, also, in the background segment of the ABC Barbara Walters Special).

Verla Morris was featured in March 2012 in a syndicated newspaper article covering the release of the 1940 census data. Verla, an avid amateur genealogist and computer whiz and all-around active new centenarian, was interviewed for her opinion on the relevance of the release of the census data, which some people oppose as an invasion of privacy. "I think it's a good thing," she told the reporter, and went on to explain why she thought so, from her perspective; she was actually included in the data.

"If I can be of help to someone, encouraging them to get off the couch and get out and move, then I'm glad to do it," Frank Shearer says. Garnett Beckman, 101, is always pleased to "help," as she puts it. She has a lovely speaking voice and does a lot of radio interviews. Elsa feels the same motivation as Frank and Garnett, but also admits to enjoying the limelight. "I had to wait until I was 100 to become a celebrity," she says, "and I love it!" Lillian does, too, although she's a bit coy about expressing it. "That's part of my Southern charm, darlin'," she says with a smile.

Rosie, 102, is miffed that he's not the only centenarian musician being featured in the media, but he's enjoying all the attention he's receiving. Rosie has played a regular Friday night gig to a packed house at a supper club in Prescott, Arizona, for the past 20 years. "Total strangers come up and give me a kiss after a set and thank me for the good time they're having. I've always liked the ladies. This is fun!" When asked how long he intends to continue, Rosie says, "As long as people want to hear Clyde McCoy's 'Sugar Blues,' or 'You Made Me Love You,' I'll live to play it for them."

The major media interest in including centenarians as role models is substantive. These aren't just social gatherings or birthday parties being covered. Elsa was again featured in a *U.S. News and World Report* article entitled "A Long Life: 7 People, Sailing Past 90 with Lots Left to Do." Garnett has appeared in a *Christian Science Monitor* article, "Redefining Longevity" (April 2010).

These are just a few examples of what is possible in our later years if we not only live long, but age well; active centenarians no longer behave like people who are 100 years old. They say they are not feeling it, either. This is good news for Boomers—and everyone—that well over two thirds of our centenarians report that they feel significantly younger than their chronological age. Many say they feel 80 or less and a few mentioned they feel mentally between 25 and 30.

"The secret is to not act your age," Marvin Kneudson, 100, offers.

The centenarians in *Celebrate 100* will tell you it's worth the effort to try to remain healthy and stay active. The fields of medicine, genetics, and technology are working overtime to come up with ways to make this feeling widely available.

Astrid Thoeing, 103, who is still working full time at her family insurance business in New Jersey as the office manager, says the trick is to not think you're old. "I don't feel old and I don't think old."

Leonard "Rosie" Ross

"Everybody wants to live to 100, but no one wants to feel old," agreed centenarian twin sisters Lois Fisher and Eloise Rogers.

THE AGE OF CENTENARIANS: A MILLION OR MORE BY 2050?

Depending on the data source referenced, there are estimated to be between 55,000 to 80,000 current centenarians in the United States, with predictions ranging from 600,000 to over 1 million by 2050.

Over the past 20 years, the ratio of those in the United States 100 and over rose from 1 in every 10,000 people to 1 in every 6,000 people. As a result, centenarians are considered to be one of the fastest, if not the fastest, growing segments of our population. Eight out of ten centenarians are women. To put this in perspective, consider that in 2012, a newborn has a 29.9 percent chance of living to be 100; someone born in 1912 had only a 0.7 percent chance of reaching the century mark. And with medical and genetic advances growing at a rapid pace, good health in later years is becoming more the norm than the exception.

Supercentenarians

Those living to very advanced age—110 and over—have been on the rise as well, thus gaining their own subset as "supercentenarians." Currently, there are an estimated 70 verified supercentenarians in the United States. No one has yet defeated the verified world record holder, Madame Jeanne Calment, of France, who lived to 122 years, 164 days.

It was our privilege to interview several supercentenarians, including the oldest, Besse Cooper, 116, who became the world's oldest living person in 2011. She turned 116 in August 2012, only the eighth person in the world to verifiably reach this remarkable age.

Walter Breuning became the world's oldest living man at 114.

The ever delightful Dr. Leila Denmark, also 114, has been a friend since turning 100.

Beatrice Farve, 113, was, at the time we met her, the second-oldest person in the United States. She was still selling Avon products until she turned 100 and drove her car until age 106.

THE WISDOM OF CENTENARIANS: AUTHENTIC—EXPERIENCE, NOT THEORY

What is best about centenarian wisdom and advice is that it is authentic: No theory—tried and true—they have lived it. Each has his or her own experience to share. They have learned about coping with life through every imaginable economic, political, social, and technological change. Their advice is timeless because the basics do not change: having enough money to live, buying a home, raising children, investing for the future. Some of their advice may be new to us and our way of thinking and differ from the way we handle our financial matters now, but timeless in the positive effect it can have on our future.

We talked to people with such disparate backgrounds as Irving Kahn, who at 107 was still working on Wall Street, to Porter Edwards, 105, who had lived all his life in South Georgia, and had earned the money to pay for the 40-acre farm on which he still lived alone by planting and picking crops.

"If I didn't have cash to pay for it, I didn't buy it,"
says Porter Edwards, 105.

Surprisingly, the amount of money people had amassed, or not, had no effect on their outlook. Again, it really boils down to the basics: do not spend more than you earn, make saving and investing an integral part of living; avoid getting in over your head with debt; don't waste money paying interest on credit cards; and plan for your future—because you just might live to be 100.

"Don't discount the possibility of living a long life," advises Lillian Cox of Tallahassee, Florida. "I did, and it was my biggest financial mistake." Lillian sold her successful business at age 65 because she assumed that she wouldn't live past age 70. Her advice is relevant to today's generation of Boomers who are charging into their 60s in record numbers, and who are facing many difficult decisions.

Lillian's resourcefulness has allowed her to continue to maintain her own home and to live a fulfilling life; she's now 106. "But still, once money is gone, it's gone."

One important aspect of money that is often overlooked is the amount of stress it can cause on a person's health and life. Centenarians had a lot to say about that. They also offered advice on work and choosing one's career: if you can, do what you love, and you will be successful.

"If you're not pleased, change. Do something you enjoy," Joe Stonis, 100, advises.

Gordy Miller of San Francisco, the world's oldest sailor, confided that sailing was the thing he enjoyed and said he only worked so he could afford to sail. It was still his passion when we visited him at age 100.

While centenarians as a group were conservative about how they handled their finances, they were not so about career and work advice and felt strongly about making the most of one's work life and career path.

"If you don't like it, you'd better get out of it," advises Mabel McCleary, 104.

The overwhelming majority of centenarians experienced meaning, purpose, and fulfillment in their work, whether it was in business or corporate America, a factory or a farm, or as an entrepreneur, salesman, or homemaker. They felt it was important because so much of one's life is spent working.

A Good Life

In addition to the questions about money and work, which we fully cover in Chapters 3 and 4, we go on to ask questions about how we can live longer and fuller lives. After all, active centenarians demonstrate that a good quality of life is attainable in later years. Along these lines, we asked, "How would you define the word *rich?*" There were various answers, of course, that ran from being a millionaire to having the love of family.

"Being rich for me is living to 100! I feel like I've won a prize," declared Gloria Posata, a new centenarian.

For Rosie Ross, the answer came easily: "Having enough extra money to buy a new trumpet," the musician said. It's the first thing Rosie did when he arrived in New York City for the Barbara Walters Special.

Often, our centenarians equated being rich with having good health: "I don't care about being a millionaire. I am a millionaire now—I'm healthy," says Bernando LaPallo, 107.

"If you have your health, you have everything," says Rosella Mathieu, 100.

Many centenarians agree and emphasize that one of the most important things a person can do in his or her life is to take good care of their health. In Chapter 2 we explore lifestyle choices people can make on their way to becoming a centenarian and take a look at what's on the horizon in genetics and medicine that will help us all live longer, healthier, and better lives.

But for now, we need to focus on the things we can control.

NATIONAL TREASURES: UNIQUE—INDIVIDUALLY AND COLLECTIVELY

As our eldest citizens, centenarians are our national treasures. There is no one else like them. Individually and collectively, they represent the wisdom, wit, and spirit of America's last 100 years and more. This status and their contributions to the building of America as we know it are being recognized on local, state, and national levels.

Manuel Vicente Osorio

Manuel Vicente Osorio became a naturalized citizen on the day before his 101st birthday. He was the first Arizonan and the 11th person in the country to become a naturalized citizen at 100 years old or older.

"It was one of the proudest moments in my life;
it was my lifelong dream to become an American citizen,"
says Manuel.

In 2012, Arizona and New Mexico each celebrated the 100th anniversary of its admission to statehood. Arizona used the celebration of centenarians as a centerpiece of its anniversary activities by hosting luncheons throughout the state honoring centenarians in their local areas. In Phoenix, on Statehood Day, February 14, the Arizona Centennial Celebration was kicked off with a luncheon honoring the 66 centenarians in attendance. The Centenarian Spirit was on full display.

We met Art Fortier as we stepped off the elevator at the Sheraton Hotel ballroom in downtown Phoenix. For a few minutes we were not sure if he was one of the honored guests or one of the attending family members. Dapper in a dark blue suit, crisp white shirt, and red tie, Art was grinning from ear to ear. "It's great to be here," he said, as we made our way through the crowd to the registration desk. It was only when he was given a boutonnière that we were certain he was a centenarian.

Finding that we were not seated with any of the centenarians, we set off to visit the other tables where centenarians and their families were gathering. To our delight, we soon found several centenarians we had interviewed for this book three years earlier. We spotted Maynard White and his daughter, Diane; Maynard was engrossed in conversation with Ralph Wilson, the centenarian seated to his left, comparing the current economic problems with those of the Depression era. We learned from Louis Reitz that he was still living in his own home, playing the organ in his living room, and riding his bicycle around the retirement community. Lucille Myers was still living in her apartment and volunteering at the senior center.

Teddy Schalow, a former switchboard operator at the Waldorf Astoria hotel in New York City, and its oldest retiree, demanded to know, "Where have you been?" We said we had been in the East and recently had lunch at the Waldorf. "How is the place?" she asked. "That was some bash they threw for me at the hotel on my 100th birthday."

We were surprised when soon-to-be-100 Verla Morris gave us her e-mail address instead of her telephone number and said, "Keep in touch." Another centenarian maneuvered skillfully between the tables on her scooter. If anyone ever doubted that active centenarians could and would keep pace with life and technology, they are wrong. And if anyone ever thought that they would outgrow their enthusiasm for life, love, and enjoyment as they aged, here was living proof they were mistaken.

Walking hand in hand through the throng, one couple stood out—he in a bright red sport jacket and she in a red skirt with a festive white blouse. "Happy Valentine's Day," she said to everyone they passed. "Happy Statehood Day," we said when we caught up with them. We mistakenly assumed the gentleman was the centenarian until his bubbly wife interrupted, saying, "I'm the centenarian! I robbed the cradle—he's 95," and off they went.

Back at our table, we enjoyed watching the video presentation of centenarians who were not at the event. One had been a Navaho Code Talker during World War II. It was interesting to hear, in his own words, how he and other Native American recruits developed the method of battlefield communication so instrumental in America's success in the Pacific.

As the program was nearing its end, we stood along a side wall, looking out over the crowd as they sang the centennial song, "I Love You, Arizona," each waving a small Arizona state flag in time to the music. In front of us was a centenarian flanked by her daughter and granddaughter, who had flown in from New York especially to attend the event with her grandmother. As the centenarian raised her arm to wave the flag, the sleeve of her jacket slipped back, revealing a series of faded numbers on her forearm—the tragic markings of a Holocaust survivor.

We were reminded, as we watched her, of Austrian psychiatrist Viktor Frankl's renowned work, *Man's Search for Meaning* (Simon & Schuster, Inc., New York, 1959, 1962, 1984), in which he, also a survivor of the Holocaust, argues that life is unconditionally meaningful and that one's sense of purpose is adaptable. "We create meaning through choices and actions as we move through life," he writes. "Meaning unfolds along with the changes in the life cycle. . . . Life can be meaningful by being an example to others."

It is instructive to recognize how much this generation of centenarians has lived through and witnessed. They are a diverse group of distinctive individuals, not only because of the lives they have lived, but also how they are living and continuing to recreate their lives at 100 and beyond. They are impressive, not only in their numbers, but in their health, vitality, activities, and interests. Every centenarian brings special knowledge from his or her life. This collective experience presents a kaleidoscope of America's history over the past 100-plus years, made up of the same events, but each represented by a slightly different story. The richness of this experience is mirrored in every centenarian throughout the country, and is the hallmark of *Celebrate 100*.

CAMEOS OF TODAY'S CENTENARIANS

Elsa Brehm Hoffmann, Entrepreneur

Elsa has never let age stop her from accomplishing her goals. At 18, she brought the love of her life home to meet her parents, assuming that since he was from the same close-knit German immigrant community, they would readily give their approval for them to marry. Bill, 10 years her senior, had just started his own roofing business in Yonkers, New York. After he left, her mother voiced her disapproval, citing the tar under his fingernails as making him unacceptable. "Ma—that's money!" Elsa exclaimed.

They married, and Elsa worked with her husband to build a successful business, using the skills she had learned working for her father in the office of his bakery supply business. When their four children were grown, the couple began to spend the winters in

Elsa Hoffman

South Florida and soon bought a small hotel, catering to fellow "snowbirds." When they moved permanently to Florida, they expanded and created a small resort, which became very popular. Elsa continued to run the resort after she was widowed at age 68, selling it in her mid-70s. With the proceeds and the money she had saved, Elsa bought a beautiful new condominium overlooking the inland waterway, and began investing in real estate.

"I've never actually retired," the vivacious centenarian says. "I handle all my own finances and several rental properties, and I continue to invest when the market is right." Elsa's drive has allowed her to live a high-quality life in her later years. She travels frequently, usually taking one of her daughters along as her companion, has a busy social life with lots of friends, and loves her new car. "I enjoy being an example to others—if I can do it, they can, too," she believes. "It makes me happy to hear people say I inspire them. I played golf until I was 98," she says proudly.

John and Marian Donnelly

John Donnelly, Bon Vivant

"I was sitting in the dentist's waiting room," Marian begins, "when this man came over and introduced himself. I thought, 'Who is this old guy?' I was in my late 60s at the time. He asked me out—can you imagine! I didn't want to hurt his feelings so I said yes, dreading a boring evening. But he picked me up in a sporty car, dressed in a sharp sport jacket, took me for an elegant dinner and then to the symphony in Sarasota. I offered to drive home—it was quite late—but he just held the passenger door open for me.

"That was the beginning of a whirlwind romance. We married in eight months and I moved into his large apartment at an upscale retirement center. John's calendar is always full, and he plans meticulously. He has his office in the sunroom, and I've turned the second bedroom into mine. We each have our own computers."

"I've always been fiscally prudent," John says, "and now I'm enjoying the benefit. But I had a chance to make a sizeable investment by buying an annuity when I was 90, so I took a risk and bet on myself.

It's paid off very nicely." Of course, John is quick to point out that his decision was well informed. "As a retired stockbroker, I have the experience to know what I'm doing. I handle all my own affairs. I enjoy going out, staying active, and being able to afford to entertain my family and friends. Marian had never been to Europe, so we spent three weeks there celebrating my 100th birthday, a couple of months in advance."

The same summer, John received a call from a producer of the *Tonight Show*, inviting him to be a guest. "That was really a surprise. I was sitting in my office one afternoon working on my bills. I was 99, about to turn 100 in the fall. I think they were interested in me because of the medals I've won playing table tennis. I am the oldest champion in the country and have been attending all the Senior Games, both nationally and in Florida, for years.

"They flew Marian and me to Burbank, California, and put us up in a nice hotel—all expenses paid (I wouldn't have gone otherwise). We had a great time. I played table tennis—he called it ping-pong—for a couple of minutes with Jay. Marian was seated in the front row, and they turned the camera on my bride. We'd been married for four years at that point, and I said we were still like newlyweds. That got a laugh from the audience and a skeptical look from Jay, but it's true."

Jack Borden, Lawyer

For Jack Borden, work and community service are their own rewards. "I always wanted to be a country lawyer," Jack says, sitting behind his large desk piled high with papers and files, "and I've been at it for over 70 years and counting. I have no intention to retire—they'll have to carry me out of here." As if to prove his point, on his desk is a small plaque that reads: "Old age and treachery will overcome youth and skill." Many of his clients are second and third generation. "Jack was my father's lawyer," one of his clients tells. "He's trusted by our family and we're lucky to have him around."

Jack Borden

"The law is a great profession," Jack says, in his easy-going, relaxed manner. "You can be a lawyer as long as people come to you for advice. If I didn't come to work every day, I think I'd be gone in six months. I enjoy helping people, and if I had to come in a wheelchair, I'd do that, too."

Interspersed with his legal career, Jack has served a four-year term as Parker County, Texas, district attorney; a four-year term as his town's mayor; and spent four years with the FBI during WWII, because he was refused enlistment in active duty due to a vision problem. When the war was over, Jack returned to Weatherford, Texas, and became a founding member of the Sheriff's Posse, a group to which he still belongs, although he points out that he no longer rides a horse. He has been a member of the Masonic Lodge for 70 years.

Along with this service, philanthropy in his community has been one of the great joys of Jack's life. The well-being of children has always been closest to his heart. Jack and his wife, Edith, lived the life of a two-career couple long before it became popular. Edith was a professor at the local college and was also a lawyer. "She was my equal in every way," Jack recalls fondly. "We never had children of our own, so we loved everyone else's and tried to take care of those in need." Jack and Edith established scholarships to the local college and were instrumental in the development of a local children's medical center.

At the age of 95, Jack was voted Citizen of the Year by the Weatherford Chamber of Commerce. Given his resume, one might think it was about time. But Jack shrugs it off and says it gives him bragging rights to be Citizen of the Year at such advanced age. He is the co-host of a local radio show at well past 100, and continues to serve as a greeter at his church, which he has done for most of his adult life. At 102, he was named America's Outstanding Oldest Worker. But his greatest honor came that same year when a new road through town was named after him. It was a blustery, cold day, but Jack was determined to cut the ribbon opening the road.

In response to the question, "What is the best thing about being 100," Jack replied: "To share with others what the past has taught me. It's also a bonus that my brother, C.B., has now hit the century mark, too."

Jack credits a positive outlook on life as one of the factors contributing to his longevity, as well as his desire to continue working. Overall, though, he says, "I think one of the reasons I've lived so long is that I love life. That's really the important thing."

Dr. Will Miles Clark and Lois Clark, Centenarian Couple

It's difficult to be serious when describing Dr. Clark and his wife, Lois, because their joy and merriment in life and in each other is contagious. They met when Lois joined Dr. Clark's dental practice in Iowa, as a hygienist and his assistant. "I knew the minute I hired her that my bachelor days were about to come to an end," Will says, smiling

Dr. and Mrs. Clark

broadly. "So we married and did the usual things—kids, house—and everything was going along smoothly until my 38th birthday when I received a telegram ordering me to report for active military duty in two weeks. They were sending me to the Pacific theatre. Imagine my surprise at this unwelcome gift! It was the last possible day that I could be drafted. We were distraught but resolved. There was nothing that could be done. Eventually, I ended up in California, waiting to ship out any day. When Lois found out that I was still in the country, she packed up the kids and immediately drove to the base to spend the last few days together. Turns out, we had several weeks. I was amazed—no one else's wife did that, that I knew of. That's my Lois!"

Lois continued to keep their life running for the next three years, until Will returned. Eventually, they retired to Arizona. "We love to travel," Lois says. "Will is a very good driver. We have a van. Sometimes we'll be sitting at the breakfast table reading the paper and get the idea we should go someplace—our son lives in California, our daughter in Colorado—and off we go, just like that."

One of a very few centenarian couples, Will and Lois are devoted to each other and loved their independence, living in their own apartment. Then one morning Lois slipped getting up and was wedged between the bed and a night table. "Will tried to free her and injured his back. They finally were able to call 911 and both spent several grueling months recovering from their injuries in a rehab center. "We were determined to return to our apartment for our 76th wedding anniversary," Will said, "although our son wanted us to move to a retirement center. I made sure Lois, who has never exercised, did all of her physical therapy, and we made it about three days before the celebration. Our children and their families came and we had a lovely time.

"Soon after, though, our son began pestering us to move, so we made it impossible for him to find a place we would agree to—we told him we had to have a place that would accommodate our king-size bed. Darned if he didn't find the perfect place! We took one look at the brand new apartment with a view of the mountains outside of Tucson, and a doorway to the bedroom large enough to fit the bed, and we said, 'Let's move.' I have a parking space for the van, and we can have our meals in the dining room if we choose.

"After we were settled in, I took up the computer," Will continues. "I hired a young man who comes once a week to give me instruction, and I work at it on my own every day. I enjoy sending e-mails, and it's amazing how I can look up things I didn't think I needed to know. We still enjoy traveling, and our son and his wife come to visit often; we always go and see something new. This past visit we went to the Roosevelt Dam, just because we'd never seen it before. We also went back to my dental school reunion in Iowa—boy, were they surprised to see me!"

Lois takes all the credit for being able to afford to live in their retirement community. "I was always very frugal with money," she explains. "Will, not so much. He would say, 'buy a new dress,' and I'd say, 'I don't need a new dress'—so I'd save the money." "With Lois being stingy and tight, we have a little nest egg now," he said, smiling.

Don and Kay Lyon—Just Cruisin'

"All days are happy days," says Don Lyon, 102. Don grew up in Carson City, Michigan, and graduated from the University of Michigan in 1929.

"I was lucky to get a job; things were pretty rough during the Depression. Young people today don't know what a depression is. The economic problems we are going through now are not nearly as bad. Those in my generation spent our 20s and 30s just trying it make it through, let alone get ahead."

With his degree in electrical engineering, Don was able to get a job with General Electric, based on the recommendation of one of his professors. "I moved to Cleveland. People all around were out of work."

Don stayed for a time, but when his father became ill he returned home to run the family flour mill. "The mill had been in our family for three generations and no changes had been made. It was obsolete. I made a lot of improvements so it could be sold. I then used the money to buy up three farms in the area, and I had several acres of top land." Knowing nothing about farming, Don hired a professional to help manage and run the farms.

Kay and Don Lyon

"When times got better, I sold them and that's what gave me the money to make my start in life. During the early 1950s the stock market was going crazy. If a person had any money to invest, you could do very well."

During WWII Don worked as a project manager in Detroit making instrumentation for aircraft, and then was offered a job in New York State, which he describes as his "dream job." I moved to Rochester and took up boating as a hobby, first sailboats on Lake Ontario and Canandaigua Lake. I joined the Rochester Yacht Club. "I would stay on my boat on weekends—I had a great life there."

Eventually, Don bought a cabin cruiser and all of his free time during good weather was spent on the water. In 1971, he retired and he and his wife moved to Florida. "The first thing I did was buy a boat, a cruiser, the largest I could get and still pull it on a trailer—it was about 20 feet. We traveled all over Florida on the inland waterways. People don't think of that, of seeing Florida by boat."

Meanwhile, Kay, a native of Columbus, Ohio, had retired to Florida with her husband in 1969. The couples belonged to the same church, and Don and Kay were widowed at around the same time.

"For a couple of years I didn't go out, except to church," Kay explains. "Don approached me, but I told him we could just be friends, and we were. Then one day after church, he grabbed me and said we should start dating. Soon he asked me to marry him, but I told him I wasn't ready. After about a year, I said to him one day, 'OK, let's get married.' The next day he took me to buy a ring. What I had never let on was that I had been smitten with Don from the first, even though he is 14 years older. Now, I admitted it. And I still am, after 21 years of marriage. Even now, if we've been apart, when I see him walk into a room I still get a thrill. It's wonderful to know I love him so much, and he loves me."

The happy couple had a big Greek wedding, and Kay introduced Don to her large, vivacious family, including her two children. "Now Don has two children and lots of grandchildren and nieces and nephews—they all love him," Kay says with pride.

And Don introduced Kay to his other love: boating. "I had never been on a boat before," Kay admits. "The first time, I asked him how he learned to drive a boat, and he said with disgust, 'You don't drive a boat, you pilot it.' That's how green I was.

But I learned, and we've had a lot of good times on large and small boats. We've taken 16 or 17 cruises."

"We've been all over," Don adds, "Morocco, a lot of exotic places. The last trip was to Greece."

"We had such a wonderful time," Kay says, taking over the conversation again. "I got to meet cousins. Don was impressed that I could speak the language, but I grew up speaking Greek because my parents were immigrants and that was the language at home. I had to learn English when I started school. On the way over we met a couple on the ship and became friends and exchanged addresses. When I happened to mention them to my Greek cousins, I learned that the woman and I were second cousins! What a surprise! I called her the next day at their hotel and said, 'Hello Cousin,' and we've visited each other here at home ever since. Life is full of surprises."

Don is a quiet, thoughtful man, a "deep thinker," as his lively wife describes him. Kay is gregarious and always cheerful. "We don't let things bother us," she says, "We enjoy life."

Don adds, "The last 20 years have been the best years of my life. We have each other, we like where we live, and we're doing all right."

A CENTURY OF PROGRESS: THEIR CENTURY

The twentieth century ushered in more changes than any other time in history, most of them progress, for example, women's right to vote; some epoch, such as Prohibition; some long overdue, such as the civil rights movement; some the result of threatening and challenging world events including two world wars; some the result of lack of regulation of the economy, for instance, the Great Depression.

In reviewing the past 100 years, centenarians have seen a technological revolution from vacuum tubes to digital transistors and ultimately the integrated circuit that drives today's small and highly complex electronic devices so prevalent in the modern world. These include the widespread use of computers and cell phones, calculators, microwave ovens, TV remote controls, VCRs, cable TV, air conditioners, all with varying degrees of sophistication.

This revolution has made possible such extraordinary achievements as putting a man on the moon and enabling the genetic research that is under way today to find keys to longevity, the "genie in the genes."

Louis Rolland, 100, says he is "very interested in the new technology and gadgets that abound." Jennie Skovich, 100, has fun playing video games, and especially likes Wii bowling. Lois Bowles, 100, enjoys surfing the web and corresponding via email as many centenarians also report.

Some centenarians, just like the rest of us, are more adept at learning technology than others, of course.

Nellie Masser is one centenarian who is not intimidated by technology and embraces it. "We've learned to use more devices in our lifetimes than there are today, albeit not as complicated as the computer. We went from an operator-based phone service and party lines to unassisted calling with a rotary phone. Then they came up with push-button phones, which were a big step for a lot of people. And portable phones—I saw a cartoon the other day where a young child asked her mother why the phone was attached to the wall at her grandmother's house."

"Looking back on it, we went from black-and-white silent movies to 'talkies,' and then to Technicolor. We went from music on records to tapes and then CDs. And we had the first televisions."

"I don't know why everyone's so surprised that I use a computer,"
Nellie Masser says. "After all, I just traded in my bingo card for a keyboard.
Now I check the stock market."

"In all aspects of life—personal, social, technological, scientific, medical, professional—there were changes within my lifetime," Dr. Karl Hartzell explains. "It wasn't just physical things and developments; customs and moral attitudes have changed, too."

In his self-published autobiography, *My First Hundred Years: A Look Back from the Finish Line,* Waldo McBurney, who lives in a small town in Kansas, enjoys a reputation as America's oldest beekeeper. Recounting the changes in modern conveniences over his century of life, he said, "I grew up on my family's farm, where life was a lot of hard work. I had a wise and thrifty mother, who would run circles around Martha Stewart in the housekeeping department. She taught me to count my blessings and to appreciate the modern-day conveniences as they came along. Her personal favorite was the electric washing machine."

"Some of us remember the early radios," a centenarian remarked. "A neighbor had the first one on our street and sometimes in the early evening he'd set it up on the porch and folks would come and set up chairs on the front lawn to listen. There weren't many programs then. His wife often served lemonade to the ladies and there was beer for the men."

"As a youngster, I fell in love with baseball and radio. I built my first radio at the age of nine. It worked! That was really exciting,"
says Charles "Cliff" Kayhart, 100.

In the popular comic strip *Dick Tracy*, his two-way wrist radio first appeared in 1948. Fascinated, scientifically inclined kids built crystal set radios and marveled at getting one station clearly in their headset. Now, a little more than a half-century later, these same "kids" can conduct a video call with their grandchildren anywhere in the world on a handheld device, in color, for free.

Foreshadowing all of these technological advances, a decade or less before our centenarians were born, Charles Duell, a lawyer, Commissioner of the U.S. Patent and Trade office (1889–1901), and a member of the New York State Assembly, predicted in 1902:

> *"In my opinion, all previous advances in the various lines of invention will appear totally insignificant when compared with those which the present century will witness. I almost wish that I might live my life over again to see the wonders which are at the threshold."*

CHARLES DUELL, "THE FRIEND," VOL. 76, 1902, P. 28

Mr. Duell was really insightful, considering all that has been developed since his forecast.

A Century of Innovation

Following are but a few examples of the innovations of the past century that we take for granted today:

1900	Modern escalator invented.
1901	The first radio receiver successfully received a radio transmission.
1902	Willis Carrier invents the air conditioner.
1903	The Wright Brothers invent the first gas-motored and manned airplane.
1905	Albert Einstein published the Theory of Relativity ($E = mc^2$).
1907	Color photography invented.
1908	Model T first sold.
1910	Thomas Edison demonstrated the first talking motion picture.
1918	Super heterodyne radio circuit invented (every radio or television uses this).
1922	Insulin invented.
1923	Traffic signal invented.
1924	Dynamic loudspeaker invented.
1926	Robert H. Goddard invents liquid-fueled rockets.
1927	Complete electronic TV system invented.
1928	Scottish biologist Alexander Fleming discovers penicillin.
1929	American Paul Galvin invents the car radio.
1930	Scotch tape patented by 3M engineer Richard G. Drew.
1932	Polaroid photography invented by Edwin Herbert Land.
1933	Stereo records invented.

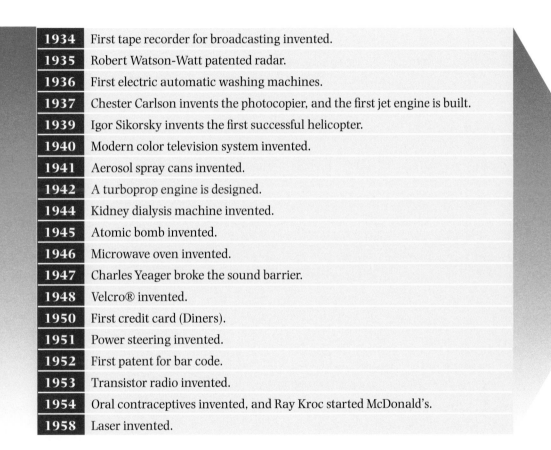

1934	First tape recorder for broadcasting invented.
1935	Robert Watson-Watt patented radar.
1936	First electric automatic washing machines.
1937	Chester Carlson invents the photocopier, and the first jet engine is built.
1939	Igor Sikorsky invents the first successful helicopter.
1940	Modern color television system invented.
1941	Aerosol spray cans invented.
1942	A turboprop engine is designed.
1944	Kidney dialysis machine invented.
1945	Atomic bomb invented.
1946	Microwave oven invented.
1947	Charles Yeager broke the sound barrier.
1948	Velcro® invented.
1950	First credit card (Diners).
1951	Power steering invented.
1952	First patent for bar code.
1953	Transistor radio invented.
1954	Oral contraceptives invented, and Ray Kroc started McDonald's.
1958	Laser invented.

1959	Internal pacemaker and the microchip invented.
1960	Halogen lamp invented.
1962	Wal-Mart founded by Sam Walton.
1963	Video disc and push-button telephone invented.
1965	Compact disc invented.
1966	Electronic fuel injection for cars invented.
1967	First handheld calculator invented.
1968	Computer mouse invented.
1969	Neil Armstrong first man on the moon.
1971	VCR and videocassette invented.
1972	Word processor invented.
1973	Ethernet (local computer network) invented.
1975	Laser printer invented.
1976	First landing on Mars.
1977	First commercial Concorde supersonic flight London to New York.
1977	Magnetic resonance imaging (MRI) invented.
1978	Artificial heart Jarvik-7 invented.
1981	IBM-PC invented.
1984	Apple Macintosh invented.

1985	Windows invented by Microsoft.
1987	Disposable contact lenses invented.
1988	Digital cellular phones invented.
1990	World Wide Web created.
1991	Digital answering machine invented.
1993	GPS satellites and positioning.
1995	DVD players and movies.
1996	First digital (filmless) cameras introduced.
1997	Wi-Fi technology.
2000	iPod introduced.
2003	First hybrid cars.
2004	Facebook launched.
2006	Electronic book readers introduced (Kindle).
2007	iPhone introduced.
2010	iPad introduced.
2011	Digital music sales outpaced CDs for the first time.
2012	Speech-operated devices in accelerated development; iPhone Siri is released as part of the iPhone 4S.
2013	Heart-powered (no battery replacement needed) pacemakers are being developed.

The balance of the twenty-first century should offer no less a spectacular array of significant advances that will help to enhance everyone's quality of life.

CHAPTER 2

The Science and Art of Living Longer and Living Better

Everybody's Doing It

ON BEING 100

INCREASING LONGEVITY

LIFESTYLE IMPROVEMENTS THROUGH TECHNOLOGY

USING COMPUTERS, TABLETS, AND SMARTPHONES

LIFESTYLE CHOICES

THE BIG THREE

HEALTHY DIET

THE BENEFITS OF EXERCISE

SOCIALIZATION AND QUALITY OF LIFE

THE IMPORTANCE OF FAMILY

INTERESTS AND AVOCATIONS

There is both a science and an art to longevity. The collective judgment of our centenarians is that living long and living well result from various combinations of genes, lifestyle, positive attitude, and luck.

Ongoing research into longevity seems to bear this out. Moreover, recent developments in technology and its use in genetic research and medicine shine a whole new light on increasing longevity—with the promise of making it available to everyone. Here, we take a look at some of the most exciting advances that will impact our well-being in the near future, that is, the "science" of longevity.

This chapter also illuminates the significance of lifestyle choices of diet, exercise, and socialization as contributing to successful aging. Through the examples, perspectives, and advice of our centenarians, we explore these factors that make up the "art" of longevity.

What we see in the lifestyles of centenarians in this book is that there is no one path to 100 and not one model centenarian. Each of us can learn from the myriad examples of those who have reached the century mark, and apply what we think would work for ourselves. And by taking advantage of new advances in technology and medicine, we have opportunities to enhance our longevity.

ON BEING 100

"Too much of a good thing is wonderful!"

Mae West

The vast majority of our centenarians say they are pleased they have lived to be 100 or more and are enjoying life. Most were surprised, though, that they had made it to the century mark. Apart from the obvious pleasure of just being alive, they responded to the question of how it feels to be 100 or more years old by making positive statements such as:

"It's wonderful to still be able to enjoy so many things."
LUCILLE BURKHART, 100

"You get to see so many new inventions, progress."
BERTE WEICHMANN, 100

*"People take an interest in you because you've lived through
so much."*
MARGARET STOWE, 102

"I like surprising people when they learn my age."
MILDRED FISHER, 100

"I enjoy having good health and being with family and friends."
ETHEL BARNHARDT, 100

"When you're 100, you can say what you want."
ELOISE WRIGHT, 100

"The best part is seeing your family grow."
ROBERT MARTIN, 100

*"Being medically and financially able to handle my life, and having
family and friends who care."*
VIRGINIA BABB, 100

"The joy of celebrating each day."
RENA LOWRY, 102

Ron Gilbert

"Read all about it!"—Newsman Ron Gilbert, 100

"At age 13, I was rejected for eighth-grade basketball because the family doctor said I had a defective heart valve. At 18, I was rejected for college physical education, because the examiner said I had leakage of the heart. At 30, I was rejected for military service; my slip said, 'Systolic murmur at apex, accentuated by exercise.'

"I shrugged it off and lived a fairly normal life for the next 40-some years, but at age 77 a cardiologist told me that I had 99 percent blockage of a coronary artery and had to have angioplasty. I scheduled it, but the cardiovascular surgeon postponed it twice because of my travel schedule and then canceled.

"So why have I lived to be 100 years old? I don't know. I have said jokingly that the only virtue I ever practiced was moderation. I smoked for 57 years, but mostly a pipe. I took a drink when I felt like it, but after a few youthful excesses I seldom took more than one or two. I ate all I wanted (when I could get it) and everything I wanted (when I could afford it). For 30 years I worked nights as a reporter in smoke-filled newsrooms.

"There were some positives. I had good genes. My parents were 92 and 94. My grandparents all lived into their 70s, and one great-grandmother lived to be 88. My mother and my wife persuaded me to eat some of the things that were good for me. My night work gave me daytime leisure that I spent working in my big garden and big yard.

"How much longer? Nobody knows. I still have my sense of humor, and I can still sing and play bridge and work crossword puzzles; I use a computer and e-mail. And I ride my motor scooter across the retirement village to visit a special lady. Life is good."

INCREASING LONGEVITY

The twentieth century saw the greatest increase in longevity in history by approximately 30 years. Improved opportunities to achieve and maintain the good health that makes longevity possible and the development of lifesaving and life-extending medical, scientific, and technical advances explain this phenomenon.

> *The current average life expectancy is approximately 77 years for men and 81 for women. At age 65 life expectancy increases to approximately 82 and 85; at age 70 it increases to 84 and 86; at age 75 it increases to 86 and 88, respectively, and so it goes. The longer we live the greater our chances are for more years and perhaps even centenarian status.*

Floyd Ellson, 100, says, "The extra years have allowed me to be around to welcome great grandchildren, and to see my dream come true: my four children and 10 grandchildren completing college. I enjoy being part of their lives; they make my life interesting. I'm glad to be here."

Centenarians express gratitude for the extra years beyond the average lifespan. Dorothy Custer, 100, of Idaho, says, "Spreading joy and laughter is what I love to do." Dorothy has had a gift for entertaining others since childhood and has participated over the years in local theatrical productions. She has written skits and made her costumes and performed in them. "I learned to play the harmonica when I was 12, and I still do. But my gift is for stand-up comedy," she tells. In her later years she joined a group called the Good Sam Traveling Club. "We go all over performing at various functions—we're in demand!" Dorothy has developed 13 characters for whom she continues to write skits and make costumes. The most popular is Granny Clampett from the *Beverly Hillbillies.*

Dorothy's starring role came at 100, when she was named Pioneer of the Year. "It's worth living long so that I get to do more of the things I love."

Fortunately, there are new medical advances available and on the horizon to help others do the same. For example, anti-aging drugs are being researched that show promise of increasing longevity, according to genetics professor David Sinclair of Harvard University: "In effect, they would slow aging."

Matters of the Heart

In 1977, Dr. Michael Heidelberger, then 89 and still working, became the oldest person ever to have a heart valve replacement. At the age of 98 he had a pacemaker implanted. These interventions not only saved his life, but also allowed him to continue to work. A pioneering researcher, he is considered the father of modern immunology. In 1989, at the age of 100, he was still in his laboratory every day at New York University Medical Center, where he continued his research until age 102.

"I've seen a lot of medical advances," Garnett Beckman, 102, says. "Within my lifetime, I've seen the development of the Salk vaccine for polio, penicillin, and antibiotics, advances in X-rays and the development of the MRI and CT scans, to name a few, and heart repair, which I've had."

In the late 1990s, Garnett, then approaching her 90s, began experiencing shortness of breath, which limited her activities such as hiking the Grand Canyon. "I'd made over 20 excursions there, starting in my mid-70s when I moved to Arizona, and I wasn't ready to quit just yet. At my age (even 20 years after Dr. Heidelberger's surgery) I had a heck of a time finding a doctor who would do the valve repair. But finally, I told him that if I was willing to take the risk he should be, too." Garnett had the operation and continued her active lifestyle. She now walks a mile every day and teaches bridge to professional women who never had time to learn.

The techniques of heart valve replacement have significantly advanced since Garnett's operation, and certainly since that of Dr. Heidelberger. It is now possible to perform this procedure in a minimally invasive manner, even on people in their 80s and 90s, giving them many more years of life. Such minimally invasive procedures increase the possibility of extending life, and the quality of life, to many more candidates of all ages.

Among other recent advances in the repair of age-related heart problems is new technology enabling the inside of the heart to be viewed in 3D. The use of this technology is helpful in resolving problems such as irregular or too rapid heartbeats or atrial fibrillation. Procedures can now be performed more quickly and safely by permitting a doctor to more clearly visualize the problem and be able to see exactly where he or she is working within the heart.

All surgeries and interventions at any age carry risks, as we know, and not everyone is a candidate for such interventions. And some are just lucky to go on without it, like Ron Gilbert.

Garnett Beckman

Like Garnett, many centenarians in our group have experienced a major medical problem in the decades leading up to 100, and often in their 90s. Yet they are reticent about discussing these challenges, and when asked will often say they don't dwell on them once passed.

Lulu Johnson, 100, is a case in point. "I believe in being positive and I love being around people," she begins. "She never complains," her daughter says, "and she strives to be upbeat at all times." But for Lulu, living to be 100 has been a series of challenges. "I've had to work at it," she confides, when asked. Along with being a cancer survivor, she has had five stents in her heart in recent years, as well as a cornea transplant "so I could continue reading, which I've always loved to do."

For Bernice Kelly, living to 100 has also been a challenge. "I enjoyed good health through my 60s," she says. "I went to the doctor once a year for a checkup and was healthy until the age of 74, at which time I was diagnosed with breast cancer. I am a survivor. In 1988 I had gall bladder surgery, in 1992 colon cancer. I am a survivor. In 1995, I had my left hip replaced. In 1999 I had cataract surgery on both eyes. My right hip was replaced in 2001, and from 2005–2010, I had pneumonia and congestive heart failure; then came diabetes in 2007. In 2009, I began having mini-strokes (TIA). My family says I have been a trooper through all of this. I do not believe in complaining about my illnesses, I am just grateful to be alive. I am a survivor. I just celebrated my 100th on March 7th (2013)."

A minority of our group, however, say they have never had a serious medical problem, and the strongest medication they take is aspirin.

Looking for the Genie in the Genes

Irma Fisher Ferguson, 104, has special bragging rights: both she and her mother lived to be centenarians, her mother to age 102. "What is so unique, I think, is that I gave my mother, Rachel Fisher, a 100th, 101st, and 102nd birthday party with family and friends, beginning in 1968. Things were more subdued then, there wasn't such a big occasion. But the whole town was impressed, of course, and happy for her. We had the party at home, with about 84 family—ranging from her children to great grandchildren—and friends, and served coffee and punch. But we did have a special cake; it was two tiers with 100 candles that was something to see. I never thought about living to be 100, but it's wonderful. I feel fine."

The Promise of Genetic Research

The potential results of genetic research are enormous and widespread. Currently, there are a number of research projects being conducted that are studying people 100 and over, looking at various aspects of centenarians' lives and genetic makeup. In demand as research subjects, centenarians are playing an important role. As one remarked, "It seems like everyone wants a sample of my DNA. I hope they find something useful."

In the very near future it is expected that definitive "longevity genes" will be identified, and that this knowledge will assist in developing new medicines and health methods to enhance longevity for us all.

Toward this end, a large research competition in 2013, the X-Prize, is being offered by the nonprofit foundation of the same name. The current prize in the Life Sciences category is $10 million for the team sequencing genomes of 100 centenarians with the most accuracy, shortest time, and lowest cost.

The Potential of Cancer Research

You would never know it to look at her, but like many of her centenarian peers, Lillian Cox, 106, is also a cancer survivor. "I was diagnosed with breast cancer in my early 90s," Lillian tells. "At that time there weren't many options and a lot of women still had mastectomies." Today, there are much less drastic procedures, and cutting-edge research that aims to provide even less invasive and more effective treatment.

A "game changer" in cancer research has taken place in recent years, thanks to the development of high-speed computers and the further development of artificial intelligence, according to Dr. Ronald A. DePinho, president of MD Anderson Cancer Center in Houston. "We can now sequence genomes of the entire tumor profile in a few hours and analyze the data for a few hundred dollars thanks to advances in computing. This is allowing us to target treatment. Also, we are in the third generation of artificial intelligence, which is helping to not only analyze the data, but draw conclusions about treatment options. The development of medicines that will trigger the power of a person's immune system is another recent advance in the treatment of cancer."

Genomics and the ability to trigger the immune system seem to be working on parallel paths. "Through genomics, if they can figure out if there is a propensity to get cancer, they can trip the immune system to stop the cancer from growing," Dr. DePinho explains. "This ability to trip the immune system may apply to other diseases that affect people in later years, such as Alzheimer's, diabetes, and heart disease."

The Fight for Sight

Deteriorating vision to the point of potential blindness is a risk as we age. Cataracts, glaucoma, macular degeneration, and other degenerative diseases challenge both the individual and medical experts alike.

Eleanor Harris

"Because of macular degeneration, I lost most of my eyesight when I was in my mid-90s," Eleanor Harris, 100, begins. "It happened gradually; my eyesight got worse and worse. At first, I had a reading machine that I used to enlarge the print to project on a screen and that was wonderful. I would write letters, checks, and read the newspaper, but after four years, that no longer helped me. I could no longer see what was on the magnified screen. That was a blow. I gave my machine to the library in hopes that someone could use it, so I had to go at it alone. It has been stressful, but there's one good thing: The doctors say with macular degeneration I will never be totally blind. I am taking comfort in that. Right now I can see forms and shapes, so I get around and I can see the white walls here at the retirement complex where I live in my own apartment. I take long walks every day and I can see people sitting or standing, but I can't see their faces. Everyone knows when they come up to me to say their name and that's how I know who they are.

"One of the hardest things in the morning is getting a shower and getting dressed. The walk-in shower here has bars to hold on to, so I feel safe. Getting clothes to match is a problem, getting the right pants and the right top. Sometimes I have problems distinguishing colors. I can see red, white, and yellow. That's why they mark the curbs with yellow. That's one color that's easy to see. I have conquered the challenge of getting dressed. I put the entire outfit on one hanger—shirt, jacket, and pants. And every night when I get undressed I put it all back on the same hanger in the closet. There are always ways to get around your difficulties.

"Fortunately, I don't need to see or read music to continue to play the piano, since I've been doing it for most of my life. My grandson says I play at nearly concert quality, but then, of course, he's my grandson," she says with a smile.

Continuing research looking to the development of gene therapy to combat degenerative eye diseases is being conducted at the Massachusetts Eye and Ear Infirmary in Boston. The object of this research is to improve clinical genetic diagnosis and the identification of new "disease genes" and research directed toward state-of-the-art clinical care for patients with genetic vision disorders. The ultimate goal, of course, is to improve and possibly restore sight to those affected. A genomic laboratory to accomplish this work in ocular genomics, as the field is called, is being built (2012).

LIFESTYLE IMPROVEMENTS THROUGH TECHNOLOGY

Bill Gates, co-founder and chairman of Microsoft, has predicted that living conditions will dramatically improve over the next 20 years due to advances in technology. "The digital revolution is just at the beginning," he said. "The pace of progress is more so than that in the 1980s when computer technology was in its infancy. Great work is being done in all the innovation sectors and at an amazing pace . . . in the lifestyle area, speech and visual recognition are improving, along with artificial intelligence."

These predictions for what's coming will make life easier as we age. What was once just imagined is becoming reality, for instance, the development of robots that can help around the house, bring objects to a person, and even do grocery shopping.

"I'd really like to have one of those robots," said centenarian Art Fortier.

A new advance in computer technology for the average consumer uses eye movements to perform a number of functions on a personal computer. It combines eye gaze with other controls, such as touch, mouse, and keyboard. These products have the potential to make computers easier to use and may be especially helpful to older people. Early examples of this technology will be available in late 2013.

USING COMPUTERS, TABLETS, AND SMARTPHONES

When it comes to computers and other new technologies, such as smartphones, many centenarians are willing to learn but some find it difficult. Nonetheless, "most of those who are interested and persist will succeed," Marvin Kneudson says confidently, obviously referring to himself as he answers a call on his cell phone during our interview.

Marvin Kneudson

"I use Skype to keep in touch with my grandsons, who live as far away as Alaska. It's great—almost like being there because we can see each other. I think more seniors should get into it. It's really easy once you get the hang of it—and it's free!" says Marvin Kneudson, 100.

Centenarian Charles Kayhart agrees that older people can enjoy new technology, as he proudly displays his iPad. (See photo in Chapter 6.)

Bernice Kelly, 100, is being introduced to Skype by her family so she can keep in touch with family members who live out of state.

Still, not all centenarians are convinced that they need to have the latest "toys," as some call them. Ruth Donaldson, who lives with her daughter near Marvin Kneudson, says, "I'd rather just pick up the phone, which I do often, and call my friends and relatives back East. I'm not into all these new electronics; they really blow my mind!"

LIFESTYLE CHOICES

When Elsa Hoffmann first learned that centenarians in other regions of the world were being studied, she said: "I don't see why researchers have to go to isolated areas of the world to try and learn the lessons of living a long and good life when we have a much higher number of centenarians here in our country to learn from, and who are very good examples. To me, that would be more relevant." (The exception is the Seventh-Day Adventist population, which is a group often studied, headquartered in Loma Linda, California. Elsa acknowledged that while it worked for them, it wasn't for her.) Frustrated and in typical take-charge fashion, Elsa decided to write and publish her own book, with the help of her granddaughter, Sharon Textor-Black. On the cover is a picture of a smiling Elsa, dressed for a formal event and being carried in by a handsome young Chippendale. Elsa has a point: there are wonderful examples of living long and living well right here in America, and many are in this book.

Elsa holds firm on the examples of America's centenarians as role models for the future of aging, adding, "You have to take into account a person's circumstances. Not everyone is dealt the same hand in life. The trick is to do the best with what you have. Not everyone has the financial resources, and they do the best they can. Not everyone wants the limelight or to look outside their family for social activities; not everyone wants to make new friends or younger friends, and they are content to spend most of their time with family. Not everyone has family and, God bless them, they are making friends and making it on their own. There's so much variety, but we all share one thing: we've made it to the century mark!"

THE BIG THREE

Along with the advances in medicine and scientific research leading to greater longevity, there is an increasing awareness of the importance that lifestyle choices play. Many centenarians are paying more attention to the role of diet, exercise, and socialization in making it to the century mark and often beyond.

Undoubtedly, there are some behaviors most of us can modify to help us live longer and healthier. We're all aware of the importance of diet and exercise and have had it drummed into our popular culture since the 1970s. Perhaps we should revisit their importance in our lives as we look ahead to our later years.

In addition, the positive impact of socialization has been largely ignored until the past few years. Current studies confirm what every older person knows: it's not healthy or happy to feel unwanted and marginalized in one's later years. Being an integral part of our families, connecting with friends, and remaining involved and interested in our communities and the world around us contributes to longevity.

Thus, what we have learned from our centenarians is that over the decades leading up to the century mark, many began to pay more attention to the positive health styles that do seem to make a difference, intentionally doing all they could to improve their chances of living longer, and maintaining a good quality of life in their advanced years. They are no longer leaving it to "good genes" or "good luck." It's a reminder for those of us who wish to follow in our centenarians' footsteps, to do the same.

HEALTHY DIET

What works for our centenarians seems to be moderation—an idea that has always been in fashion, for those who can do it. Our centenarians have had the discipline and wherewithal to live their lives accordingly. While some enjoy a glass of wine or a cock-tail, they are quick to add that it is never in excess; while many say they do not follow a particular diet (such as vegetarianism), in general they are not big eaters and most are of average weight or less. Very few are obese, and none in our group.

Right-Sized, Not Super-Sized Meals

In 1960, when centenarians were in middle age, the average individual weighed 20 to 30 pounds less than those in their middle age today. While there are many differ-ent schools of thought on this increase, three factors seem to be most important. The introduction of high-sugar, high-fat fast foods and increased portion sizes—the more is better mentality—and less physical demand on an individual's routine, as walking has been replaced by driving, housework has become easier, and the workplace has become more automated.

"The answer (to being overweight) to me is simple: downsize your supersize meals," says Astrid Thoenig, 103.

"For those who recall the dinnerware and glasses of the 1950s and 60s, they were much smaller than their counterparts today. A dinner plate was closer in size to today's salad plates, and wine glasses were a third of the size of those in use today. Take a look at your wedding china if you still have some; you'll see what I mean. Instead of worrying about what diet to be on, why not just eat fewer calories. It works."

Several studies are investigating the connection between calorie-restricted diets and longevity, with varied results. But this is not the extent to which our centenarians refer. In general, they will say: eat a balanced diet and eat sensibly. Besse Cooper, 116, the world's oldest woman in 2012, advised, "Don't eat junk food!" The majority of our centenarians share her view.

Bernando LaPallo

For Some, an Extreme Diet Is the Key

Some centenarians, like Bernando LaPallo, take a holistic approach to life. At 107, when we first met him, he looked and acted 30 years younger. "I believe in a raw food diet, much of the time; sometimes vegan, but nothing beyond vegetarian," he reports. "I've been eating like this for most of my life."

Bernando also believes in the importance of dietary supplements to help him remain healthy and vital. If anything, he seems more active two years later at 109 than ever. In the interim, he's written a book, *Age Less/Live More: Achieving Health and Vitality at 107 and Beyond*, and is working on another. He gives talks on the benefits of a vegan/vegetarian diet, and has an active web site maintained to spread his message. His vitality is amazing.

Heart-Healthy Diet

For people who have heart disease, recent research shows that a heart-healthy diet can make a world of difference, even in later years.

Former President Bill Clinton, for one, has been outspoken about his change to a low-fat, primarily vegan diet. Proponents of a vegan or vegetarian diet say it helps with weight loss, is anti-inflammatory, and beneficial in lowering cholesterol and blood pressure.

A recent large-scale international study was conducted to assess the benefits of a heart healthy diet. There were 31,546 adults ages 55 and over in 14 countries, enrolled in two separate clinical trials of blood pressure–lowering medications. These subjects were considered high risk for heart attack, stroke, or other heart-related problems and were shown to have significantly benefitted from a heart healthy diet with an emphasis on eating fruits and vegetables, fish, and nuts. Mahshid Dehghan, PhD, a research associate at McMaster University in Hamilton, Ontario, Canada, said, "Many people with heart disease may be under the mistaken impression that taking their medication is enough to reduce their risk."

In early 2013, the *New England Journal of Medicine* reported on a large-scale study showing that a so-called Mediterranean diet, featuring the use of olive oil and nuts, along with fruits, vegetables, eggs, dark chocolate, whole-grain cereals, fish and white meat skinless chicken and turkey, reduced the incidence of heart disease.

Maurine Furney, 100, says, "My lifelong emphasis on good nutrition has contributed to excellent health and an active centenarian lifestyle."

Maurine lives independently and recently attended a high school alumni get-together. "Of course, I was the oldest one there."

Dr. Frank Shearer

The Seventh-day Adventist Diet

Dr. Frank Shearer, 105, points to the studies conducted on the lifestyle of Seventh-day Adventists by Loma Linda University in California, his alma mater. "It has been found that those who follow the Seventh-day Adventist lifestyle live several years longer than the average American.

"We eat only a vegetarian or a vegan diet, and are strict about taking our Sabbath (Saturday) as a day of rest and renewal, faith, and prayer. I think the day of rest and a break from everyday stresses is as important as the diet. We also believe in keeping physically active. However, younger members are not as strictly adhering to this regimented diet, so we'll see if that makes a difference."

Dr. Shearer practiced medicine as a country doctor for 50-plus years. During these years he found time for horseback riding, camping, fishing, flying (as a private pilot), and water skiing, a sport he took up in the 1930s and still enjoys on occasion.

THE BENEFITS OF EXERCISE

When it comes to exercise, despite what is now known about its importance in contributing to good health, there is no consistency among our centenarians. However, we have found they are trending toward the contemporary view that exercise is important to health and vitality. More centenarians are exercising, even if they began later in life. Of the late bloomers, around age 75 seems the mean, and they continue to do so. As Louise Calder, 100, says, "I don't leave my bedroom each morning—not even for breakfast—until I've done my half-hour of stretches" (later she walks at least a half-mile). Centenarians are "hitting the gym," too, and engaging in strength and resistance training, along with the stationary bike; many have them at home. The treadmill is the one exercise device they shy away from. An established and frequently referenced study at Tufts University in Boston has found that older people, even those 100 and over, can benefit from strength training.

*The late Dr. Robert Butler, known as the father of geriatric medicine,
said as far back as the 1980s: "If there were only one prescription I could
give to my patients it would be to exercise."*

Katherine "Kit" Abrahamson—Dancing at 80 and Beyond

Katherine "Kit" Abrahamson took up dancing when she turned 80 and continued until six months before her 105th birthday. Her favorite dance is tap but the group she belongs to, The Cape Ann Seniorettes, specializes in line dancing. Kit believes the twice-weekly dance lessons for over two decades have kept her agile and healthy, and certainly happier.

A lifelong resident of Gloucester, Massachusetts, Kit is one of 14 children from a close-knit Irish family. "I've learned that family is very important, of course, but you also need to have outside friends, or you'll be boring. My best friend is a member of our dance group in her 80s. She's tall, I'm short; of course, they call us Mutt and Jeff, but we don't mind—it's all in good fun." Kit admits to still getting stage fright even after 20-plus years of recitals. "Once a year we have a large recital and everyone's family comes, of course, and so do lots of town folks. And every year I have butterflies in my stomach, afraid I'll forget a step, but I never do. I guess it keeps me on my toes, so to speak. My great granddaughter Katie—my namesake—took up dancing when she was 10. She began taking dance lessons at the same studio I go to, and she learned the line dance steps. She looked so cute in her cowgirl boots and hat, and we danced together for several years at recitals. We were quite a team, just 90 years apart!

"Our dance group performs at events in the area and community events and at retirement homes. Most of the residents there are younger than I am."

George Blevins—Kegling Champ

George Blevins is a bowling champion at age 100. He is a regular participant at the National Senior Games and the only 100-year-old bowler in the over 75 class.

George Blevins

George has won two national bowling singles tournaments. He is one of two centenarians regularly participating in the games (the other is John Donnelly, the table tennis champ). George also competes in the Indiana State Senior Singles Tournament.

Attracted to bowling at the early age of seven, George continued to bowl while an industrial engineering student at Purdue University, as well as during his long career as a special assignment engineer for International Harvester. "One year I was the captain of five different teams," he says proudly. "But some years I had trouble making it back home to stay active on any team, and I really missed it. I traveled a lot for my work, driving all over Indiana. When I retired, I took up bowling full time. I love it.

"In my early days we had natural wood lanes and pins. Oil patterns made it difficult to keep the ball on a line to the pocket. 'Pin stickers' labored for 10 cents a game, picking up the pins and resetting them for the next shot. It was hard work. Score keeping was done by hand using pencils on large sheets of paper. It was not like using the modern automatic score keepers of today. I learned to add the score in my head.

"I never thought about living to 100. No one in my family lived particularly long that I knew of. I thought of myself as just an average guy. Then, when I was in my 90s, I continued bowling, being active, and living on my own.

"I realized that I was doing more than most 90-year-olds do
ordinarily, so I started to think of myself as something special, and then
I hit 100—wow!"

"I still drive and bowl two to three times a week. I bowl in a league on Monday and practice on Wednesday and Thursday." George credits "clean living and a steady diet of 10 pins" for at least part of his longevity and robust health. "The rest is a mystery," he says. "But I'll take it."

Elmer Askwith

A few centenarians, Elmer Askwith for one, still grow their own vegetables and at the same time get vigorous exercise. Elmer is very proud of his large garden and says, "I've been duking it out with the clay soil of northern Michigan for over 60 years." To do so, he has created his own composting system and nourishes his soil each year. "I've rigged a composter to do it."

Elmer says he has always been industrious and inventive in a practical way. He lives alone in the house he built for himself and his wife many years ago, and until recently heated only by a wood stove, with wood he carried in himself. "I made a special backpack as I got older so I could carry it easier," he tells. Elmer enjoys building and fixing things, and finding ways around everyday challenges. It's a trait he developed long ago and it has served him well over the years.

"I was born on a farm in upper Michigan in 1911," Elmer begins. "Like our neighbors, our family was long on love and short on cash. We didn't have two pennies to rub together. When I was seven, I decided I wanted a violin. My father agreed, so long as I earned the $7 it would cost to order it from the Sears and Roebuck catalog, as most everyone did in those days. They carried everything from toys to clothes and washing machines—heck, you could even buy a house from the catalog and put it up yourself. I knew people who did that.

"Anyway, I found out that the township was paying 10 cents, a princely sum, each for a rat tail, as a means of holding down the rat population in the area. So I tried various methods of catching them, with little success.

"Then one day I decided to build a trap using the rain barrel—cut a hole in the top, put a few kernels of corn on the lid, and when the rat came for them, he fell into the barrel and drowned.

"Pretty soon I had my violin, and after torturous practice (my father said it almost killed him) became so good at it that by high school I started a band. We played school dances, at church functions, sometimes in people's homes at parties. We played the fox trot, waltzes, and square dances; it's how I met my wife. People would come from as far away as 20 miles to hear us play and dance to our music—we were that good!

"We married in 1932 during the Depression. It was awful. Men would do about anything to get work. I was lucky to get a job as a fire ranger and spent six summers, 10 hours a day, 7 days a week, sitting atop a 40-foot fire tower with binoculars, waiting to report a fire, which a lot of the time I did. But much of the time was just sitting. I would play my violin, but I also started designing my future home.

"Eventually, I got a job at the Sault Ste. Marie locks and worked there for 35 years, retiring as a lock master.

"When I could finally afford to build our home, I bought 10 acres from the township and dug the basement myself in the same hard clay. I dug it by hand, sometimes using a sledgehammer to break up the clay. There were many delays, and I had to try three times because the rain would keep washing in the hole. It wasn't until after the cement was poured that I noticed that the hole wasn't square—so I built a crooked house to fit it.

"The most frustrating point in my life came shortly after the house was finished. No sooner had we moved in when the town came to me and said they needed part of my land to build a schoolhouse. Unfortunately, the part they wanted was where I had just built the house! So I had to dig another basement down the road, and then rig up logs to move the house on. I did, and I'm still living here today."

Maintaining Independence

A surprising number of centenarians in our group live independently. About 35 percent live either in their own home or apartment or in an apartment in a retirement center. Most were rightfully pleased to be doing their own housework, which they count as exercise, and of taking care of themselves.

Elmer Askwith

Mattie Bell Robinson, 100, says, "I continue to live independently in my own home and I still plant a garden and can food for the winter months."

Mental Exercise

In addition to staying physically active, our centenarians are acutely aware of the importance of keeping their minds active. Ron Gilbert plays bridge, as do many others; Louise Brooks loves crossword puzzles, another popular mental exercise; and most read the newspaper daily. Others pursue hobbies, including artwork and crafts, like Bonnie Hernandez, who loves to crochet. And, of course, there are the techies who love using their computers, e-mail, smartphones, and iPads. Some are still taking classes at local colleges, community colleges, at their senior centers, retirement homes, and churches.

"My husband and I performed at the Metropolitan Opera as supernumeraries (extras) for over 50 years. I still live in New York and my current hobbies include 300-plus piece puzzles and working on my iPad," says Kitty Slesinger, 100.

Stay Sharp, Stay Young

Dr. Herbert Bauer, 102, has been known to read an entire book almost every day. "He's incredible," a friend says. "He's kept on learning throughout his life." When asked what has been his key to success through a lot of different times and difficult circumstances, the resourceful centenarian credits persistence and a positive attitude.

A few days after completing his medical degree in Vienna, Austria, in 1936, Dr. Bauer abruptly left the country just after the Nazi invasion. "I escaped by jumping out a window just as the Nazis were pounding on the front door. That was the only way to get out alive, and I had the worst possible classification: Liberal!

"I spent a few years in England before coming to America in 1940," he tells. While in London Dr. Bauer helped find jobs for people who escaped from German-occupied countries, and met his wife, Hanna, in the process. They settled in California, in the San Francisco area, where Dr. Bauer finished his medical internship while working as a nursing assistant. "You do what you have to do," he says pragmatically. Dr. Bauer started a public health career about 70 years ago near Sacramento, and served as Yolo County's public health director from 1952 to 1971. He is credited with having created the health department there. "I started it from the ground up—I knew I could make something of it." The desire to help the underserved and underprivileged has been a central tenet of his life.

"I even have a new building named after me. The Herbert Bauer M.D. Health and Alcohol, Drug & Mental Health Building, located in Woodland, California, the capital of Yolo, County."

"The supervisors told me this is the second-largest building in Woodland,"
Dr. Bauer said. "The biggest is the county jail. I'm No. 2."

Later, he joined the faculty at the University of California, Davis Medical School, as a Clinical Professor and has continued lecturing there from time to time since retirement and even after becoming a centenarian.

Over the years, Dr. Bauer improved his academic credentials by adding a master's degree in public health from the University of California at Berkeley, and, at the age of 61, a child psychiatry certification from UC Davis. (His wife was a clinical psychologist.)

He has enjoyed an active retirement. At age 99, Dr. Bauer traveled to Europe, including a river cruise on the Danube. "I stayed a short time in Vienna, where I visited the house in which I was born. It was still standing there and the window through which I escaped was open. The people I met in Austria were quite friendly but seemed unaware of their past history. For instance, they took me to the high school from which I graduated and asked me what I remembered. Wanting to be as kind to them as they were to me, I did not tell them that during the years prior to the German invasion, the Nazi party had been active in their country. Nor did I tell them that what I remembered from high school was the Nazis coming in and beating us out of the classroom. What I really enjoyed in Vienna, then and always, was their glorious music, their Alps, and their Apfelstrudel. Don't tell me I am not fair!

"I have always stayed active in local health committees," he said. At 99, "I took up dance, joining the dance theater in Davis. I also taught a course at a lifelong learning center, Sex and the Law."

About growing older, Dr. Bauer advises maintaining an active social life. "It is important as we age. I don't think there has to be a cutoff—at 65 you're old. You're not old. Continue doing things you enjoy and are interested in throughout your life, no matter what your age, both in your personal relationships and avocation. Keep trying new things that interest you. Life isn't over; do something else that uses your talents after you retire from your main work, but plan ahead. Don't just wake up one day and say, 'What am I going to do now?'"

Dr. Bauer continues to live in his home, has a multitude of friends, and swims "most days" in his pool.

SOCIALIZATION AND QUALITY OF LIFE

"Social gatherings and a good sense of humor have helped
me live to 100," says Winnie Harmon, 100.

As mentioned earlier, socialization is one of the three components to a healthy lifestyle, along with diet and exercise, that contribute to a good quality of life in later years. As we are reminded by our centenarians, it's not just how long we live that matters, but also how well. The examples of how they continue to interact with family, friends, and their communities show us that achieving a good quality of life in later years is possible. And it is never too late for romance.

Numerous studies have confirmed what our centenarian experts say: that socialization is as important to maintaining health and a good quality of life in advanced years as are diet and exercise. The feelings of loneliness and isolation are the culprits, it seems, that rob an elder of feeling well; not the physical act of living alone, as many family members and social workers fear. In fact, a Harvard study posits that an 80-year-old living alone might be stronger and healthier than someone of the same age who can't manage on their own.

Clarence Weinandy, 100, who is known as Andy, can attest to this. "I live alone in a close-knit neighborhood in Florida," he says, "but I'm never lonely. My neighbors are my friends. They look in on me, keep tabs on me; we go out together, they invite me to dinner . . . they're terrific. I was born and raised in Ohio. My mother was very strict but loving. She had several basic rules that she pounded into me. One was: 'A person who can't amuse himself is poor company for others.'"

Social Networking

The era of the computer, cell phones, and now smartphones, Facebook, and Twitter allow older adults to keep pace with contemporary life and be involved with each other, staying up to date with current events, making new friends, and continuing contact with multiple generations in their families. These devices help overcome not only social barriers but physical impediments, distances, inclement weather, and not driving. They also help manage financial tasks for those who have learned to use them, in general making life easier.

At 100, Miriam Samson says she is "active on the computer to be current with the changes in technology." She's experimenting with making new friends using social media, but relies mostly on e-mail for writing to her friends. "I even send condolence letters now by e-mail," she says.

Some centenarians who were users of computers in their 80s and 90s have chosen to help share their knowledge with their peers. Centenarian Bill Miller began using a computer at age 89, given to him by his sons. He was then left to his own devices to learn. "I found a new direction in life," he says. "Once proficient, Bill volunteered at the local library and taught seniors how to use the computer and navigate the Internet. He has been recognized by the Baltimore County Public Library for his years of dedicated service.

At the age of 99, then a widower, he met a special friend, Jeanne, "who has given me a new spirit and meaning to my life," he says. Valentine's Day is their favorite celebration. Bill enjoys mathematical games and tricks, which he likes to play on his friends. What keeps him young at heart, he believes, is his interest in continuing to learn new things.

*With his zest for life and contemporary view, Bill says "I am happy
being a good example to my two sons, five grandchildren,
and three great grandchildren."*

Not surprisingly, recent centenarians are more likely to be interested in learning and using technology. Walter Kistler, 100, says "I do everything on my computer including making greeting cards. My wife Sally, who is 98, also has her own computer and enjoys corresponding via email."

Others, as with Bill Miller, have been using computers for several years leading up to the century mark. And for some centenarians, like Verla Morris, the burgeoning use of technology in their careers has made them more inclined to keep current with its use after they retired.

Love and Relationships

Some people find it surprising that in later years romance still blooms and may be amazed to see couples in their 70s and over on a romantic first date. What we've learned from centenarians is that people don't outgrow their desire for love and companionship. There are numerous examples of second or even third marriages occurring later in life—70s, 80s, and 90s—such as John and Marian Donnelly, and Don and Kay Lyon. Yet some centenarians, such as Will and Lois Clark, and Jon and Ann Betar, are still married to their original spouses (for 75 years or more).

Bess Pettycrew and Paul Olson

For Bess Pettycrew, 101, meeting Paul Olson, 103, "is the best part of being a centenarian."

Bess was living in a retirement center in the Midwest town near where she was born and raised. Paul had been living on his family farm, which he'd been running all his life. After losing his wife, he decided to move into town to an apartment at the active retirement community. "On the first day there, I was shown to a dining table and introduced to a few

Paul Olson

of the other residents. I was seated next to a woman by the name of Bess. We soon discovered we had gone to high schools in neighboring towns and that she had graduated just a couple of years after I did in 1925. We struck up a conversation and have been together every day since," he says with a broad smile. "It's nice when you find someone who grew up in similar circumstances and around your own age. We have a lot in common."

Paul began playing the saxophone and played in the school band and in a dance band with some friends. Later, he also played sax in the town band and a few more local dance bands over the years. "I was never good enough to play professionally," he says, candidly. "I don't know why we never met earlier," Bess muses. "I went to many of those functions."

Paul has continued playing with a group of friends at the retirement center in what they call the Just for Fun Band. "Most of the other members are 20 years younger. We entertain regularly at nursing homes in the area and, of course, play for dances and functions at our retirement center. People really enjoy the old tunes, the ones they grew up with, and I remember them all." But he is quick to add, "Our playlist also includes more current favorites, too."

"I like his music," Bess adds. "He makes things a lot of fun."

Betty Lucarelli

"After I was widowed in my late 70s, my cousin invited me to come to Florida to visit and escape the New Jersey winter. He lived in an apartment in a large retirement community that had guest rooms for visitors. On the first day, we went to play golf, and he had a friend with him from Ohio, who had also been invited to visit and was staying with him in his apartment, unbeknownst to me.

"We played nine holes and had a pleasant time, and I didn't think anything more of it. Later that afternoon I was invited down to his apartment for cocktails, and there was Ernst again. We had more of a chance to talk and get to know each other. I learned that he had recently lost his wife. The more we talked, the more we found we had a lot in common—we were of the same Italian heritage, the same religion, and liked many of the same activities. And Ernst enjoyed good food—and I'm a good cook!

"The next day he asked me out for dinner and we talked some more—and kept on talking. By the end of my two-week visit, we had decided that he would come home with me to New Jersey. He met my kids and my friends; within a few months he sold his home and we married and lived in my home in New Jersey. The next year, we decided to move permanently to Florida.

"We bought a home and made new friends. (Ernst is five years younger.) We love to dance, go out, entertain, and we have traveled worldwide. On Sundays, I pick up a friend who doesn't drive and we go to church in the morning; Ernst has some 'quiet time' to read the papers. When I come home, I prepare a big Italian meal (although I admit I do use jarred sauce now, but I doctor it up). Then friends and neighbors drop by for dinner—they don't need special invitations. Anyone who wants to can come. We have a full house and a lot of fun."

Ernst adds, "Betty does all the cooking. You don't mess with Betty in the kitchen. That's her domain."

"We have a good life," Betty concludes. "I never thought I'd be so happy again."

Relationships with Friends

For Helen King, 100, belonging to the Red Hat Society and staying active in their many events and functions provides an active social life. "The Red Hat Society is one of the largest social organizations in the world, with chapters everywhere. Unlike some organizations for women, there are a lot of older women here and age is not a barrier. In fact, it's encouraged," she says.

For others, such as Lillian Cox, it's belonging to the garden club and other traditional women's organizations. Marion Rising, 101, says "I enjoy playing word and board games, being with friends, and doing my volunteer work."

Teddy Schalow is a fixture at her local senior center, which she helped to found many years ago when she moved to Arizona from New York. "They needed a lot of things here; it was pretty quiet. So I thought I'd liven it up a bit. After we got the space and had the center up and running, I began organizing parties for every possible occasion—we had dances, buffets, brunches, movies, you name it." She volunteered into her mid–90s. "Now I come and let them wait on me," she says good-naturedly. "Everybody knows me here. They come up and give me hugs. It makes my day. Everybody should have a hug now and then."

Teddy Schalow

Teddy still drives her car to the center, smartly dressed and wearing her trademark heels. "You'll never catch me in flat shoes," she says as she opens her closet door to display at least 40 pairs of midsize heeled pumps. "Not even around the house."

For Maynard White, 101, who lives with his daughter in her home, it's the senior center and his church that provide outside socialization. "I don't want to sit around the house all day," he says. "I feel the church has, in particular, given me a desire to help people in times of need, and I try to contribute my time to them. It's a good foundation for living a good life, and I enjoy the people there."

For Dick Morris, 102, fraternizing with friends at the retirement center where he lives in his own apartment has kept him socially engaged. "I go along on all the outings and help the activities director with the people in wheelchairs, getting them in the van, pushing them in restaurants, the mall, the movie theatre—we go a lot of places, and I want to make sure as many people can come along as possible. I help stow the wheelchairs in the hold if we are taking a bus excursion."

Dick was born and raised in Emporia, Kansas, and spent his formative years on the family farm. As a teenager he longed for adventure and worked for a year painting houses and saving his money. "By 19, I wanted to see mountains and the ocean—something more than the flat plains of Kansas. I traveled with a friend. When we got to Colorado we decided to keep on going and made our way to San Francisco. I loved the beauty of the West. We looked for work all along the coast, down to Los Angeles. Finally, as luck would have it, we ended up in Seattle where I got a job at the Fisher Flour Mill on Harbor Island. I stayed there for over 20 years. I married the widow of one of my good friends at the mill; she had a son and a large extended family in the area. They became my family.

"In 1941, we bought our first house and later sold it and bought a four-unit apartment building. In 1950, I quit the mill and bought a 65-acre resort on the waterfront. My wife, Alice, was the greatest business partner a man could ask for. For us, the resort was nonstop work. After 10 years, we'd had enough. We sold it and bought a house, fixed it up, and sold it in three months. That was successful, so we kept on doing it—buying fixer-uppers and selling them. That started my new career in real estate, which lasted 17 years. At 65 I decided it was time to learn to play golf, and we bought a mobile home and became snowbirds in Arizona and Southern California. It was a good life; in summer months we continued in real estate." Dick's motto is: "Learn to be contented, but never satisfied. In other words, never settle—always strive for improvement."

Volunteer Work and Community Service

With or without family members for companionship, staying active in a worthwhile cause can bring a sense of purpose and camaraderie. Centenarian Martha Harrison, for example, spends her time knitting caps for premature babies at a local hospital, although she's never had children of her own. "So far, I've made 1,400, and the hospital gave me a plaque for my volunteer work. Whenever there is a new baby on the way in my family—my nieces' and nephews' children—I start knitting. It's nice nowadays because you get to know if it's a boy or girl in advance. I used to make a lot of yellow caps and bassinet blankets."

Miriam Krotzner

Miriam Krotzner, 100, of Prescott, Arizona, begins by saying, "I'm alone in the world except for my church and my friends." Miriam and her first husband did not have children, and he died many years ago. Miriam has been on her own, living in her home, driving her car, and taking care of herself for a long time. Originally from Phoenix, she and her husband married at the age of 22 and ran a gas station and a small general store on the western outskirts of Phoenix. "We were like what would now be thought of as a convenience store," she says in her chipper, upbeat way. "We lived in a small house across the street. It was his family's business, and he was supporting his widowed mother and nine younger siblings." When her husband became ill and could no longer work, she took a job at a "dime store" and enrolled in classes at a local college, "mostly typing and bookkeeping," Miriam says.

After a three-year illness, her husband succumbed to tuberculosis. Miriam took an office job in Phoenix, where she met her second husband. They moved to Seattle, where she worked for many years for Northwest Airlines as a reservationist. "I was using one of the earliest computers," she recounts. "It really was a new field, as was the entire reservation industry. It was exciting. I loved living in Seattle." However, after her husband retired, they moved back to Arizona, to Prescott, for his health, which had been compromised by injuries sustained during World War II. Miriam was again widowed in 1990.

Miriam began volunteering at the VA hospital in Prescott, where long after retirement age she remains active. She also became very involved in her church and attends weekly Bible studies. "This is important to me," she says. "It's important to make friends—especially younger friends—when you're alone and older. My friends are all 20 or more years younger, but they treat me as their equal." Miriam is friendly, witty, and thinks and speaks at lightning speed. She also has a wonderful recall of people she's met.

"I have read the Bible entirely through three times," she says. "You need to keep re-reading it and studying because you can't remember all that's there." Miriam says she reads several passages and special prayers each day, saying that it grounds her. "Some days, I read more."

At 96, she fell on New Year's Eve. "I was getting out of my car at the VA to go in to help serve a special dinner to the residents, and I slipped on the ice. I was rushing. I broke my hip, and it's bothered me ever since, so now I use a cane for support, but I keep going!"

Never one to dwell on the negative, she counters brightly. "Did you know that Genesis 6:3 tells us that God has intended us to live for 120 years? I believe it."

Mr. D

For Fermin Montes de Oca, 105, doing for others brings him a sense of satisfaction. In his full life, he has always found time for volunteering, but nothing has meant more to him than the Country Store he opened and runs at the retirement center where he has lived for several years in Florida. His store provides some necessities and lots of treats for the residents, including his very popular Mr. D's Popcorn. For years, he has risen each morning at 4:30 to make the fresh popcorn to sell during the day at his store, which is staffed with other volunteers. At the end of each day, he gives the proceeds of the store's sales to the hospice workers to buy things to help people in need.

"The people depend on me," he says of his rigorous schedule. It was even difficult to get him to take time off to celebrate his 105th birthday. When asked, he can't explain his desire to help others. He says he's always been this way.

Born in Tampa, Florida, he and his older brother went to work when he was 10, shining shoes outside a cigar factory. They charged a nickel for black shoes and a dime for brown. After shinning 12 to 15 pairs of shoes, young Fermin would race home and proudly give all of his earnings to his mother.

When he was 15, his father moved the family back to his native Cuba and Fermin went to work for a cigar factory. He met the love of his life at an early age, and they were married for 76 years. They moved to New York, where Fermin got a job as a barber at the Waldorf Astoria Hotel. Gary Cooper became one of his regular customers and they developed a rapport. Cooper nicknamed him "Shorty."

Eventually, he and his wife moved back to Florida, where "we had two sons, built a house, and lived happily," he says. "I went to work for a cigar factory and stayed for 39 years, but I never smoked a cigar or cigarette."

Joe Stonis

Joe Stonis, 100, is a man who was ahead of his time in Florida when he retired there over 30 years ago with his second wife, Doris. His chosen area, he recalls, "looked like a desert when I first saw it. I first noticed the ugly terrain from the plane, and by the time we landed I had decided that if this was going to be where I would spend the rest of my life, I had to do something to improve it!" Improve it he did, by becoming an advocate for green space and beautification. He turned the barren landscape into what is now a lush town on the Gulf Coast.

Born in Newark, New Jersey, with a career in the chemical industry, Joe had lived in several parts of the country, "wherever they sent me," he says. "I had no experience in landscaping, but I began planting trees, so much so that I became known locally as the 'tree man.'"

Joe began several civic initiatives to plant trees, to landscape the area, and eventually to advocate against the encroaching development in favor of a balance of green space. He has been spectacularly successful in his pursuit to bring green, beautiful open space to his corner of paradise. "If there's a tree being planted here, I've likely had something to do with it," he says proudly. Over the years, the trees Joe had planted initially have matured and it all looks natural now, "like it's always been here," he says.

Joe Stonis

And that's just the way he likes it. "But I don't stop. I'm always coming up with something new to add to the beauty of this place." Joe's energy is amazing!

Others have recognized that these trees and greenery didn't just happen by themselves, and Joe has received numerous honors from the community and the state. At age 91, he was the oldest recipient of the National Arbor Day Foundation award for his work at the community level. He adds this to his array of trophies won for his hobby: fishing, both fresh and saltwater. And along the way he's written a book called *Slices of American Pie*, which he published at age 98. He's now at work on another.

Joe is a wonderful example of the rich opportunities that can await a person in his or her retirement years. "Before I moved here, I never gave a thought to trees," he says. "It just suddenly came to me that I have to do this. It's really kept me going, interested and involved in the community and in other people."

THE IMPORTANCE OF FAMILY

All centenarians who enjoy the closeness and attention of family rave about the difference it makes in their lives. They love being in touch with younger generations, watching them grow and have children of their own. As Pauline Copeland, 100, says, "We have five generations of Copelands now. It's wonderful to watch them grow and to be surrounded by my children and their spouses, my grandchildren and their spouses, great grandchildren, and great great grandchildren. We often all get together and sing and just have a good time. Of course, I miss my husband Dewey and my beloved son Albert not being here to share in these joyous times."

"I have made my family the most important thing in my life by showering all of them with love and respect and most of all the best homemade baked goodies and food!" says Esther Laufer, 100.

Centenarians who are considered the matriarchs or patriarchs in their families derive a sense of fulfillment and satisfaction from their role. They consider it an important responsibility to pass on their wisdom, knowledge, and family history to their descendants, either through written memoirs or stories and oral histories they share.

Karl Drew Hartzell

Karl Drew Hartzell, PhD, has had a long and distinguished career as a successful and respected professor, dean, and administrator in higher educational institutions. He also held a high-level administrative position at the prestigious Brookhaven National Laboratory. During WWII, he was appointed to the New York State War Council. Karl has lived the life of a brilliant intellectual, and continues to do so at age 102.

But it is not his impressive career or his many accomplishments—or even his current active lifestyle—that matters most to him. "Being a devoted father is my greatest role in life," he says. "I credit my three sons for my longevity. Having children who are active and make it possible to think with them as they face their own evolving life concerns has been a factor in the quality of my life. My three boys and I have remained close. I travel (from his home in Florida) to visit them often (in the Northeast).

"I lost my father at the age of 10; he was a minister in the Methodist church. We moved to Massachusetts from California to live with my mother's parents; she never remarried. Thus, my grandfather became the central father figure in my life. Were it not for him, I think I would have followed my father's side of the family into the ministry. Both sides of my family were religious refugees to America: my mother's family, the Drews, arrived in Plymouth, Massachusetts, in 1640; the Hartzells arrived in Pennsylvania near Philadelphia around 1730. I remain keenly interested in the study of religion to this day.

"My grandfather was a Boston lawyer, and he encouraged me in another direction. It was his view that to succeed in life I needed to excel at academics. I attended Wesleyan University in Middletown, Connecticut, made Phi Beta Kappa (I was the only one with three athletic letters to do so—tennis was my best sport, and I was captain of the tennis team), and went on to Harvard graduate school for my PhD in history. It was his

Karl Hartzell, PhD

financial support, as well, that allowed me to do this. I finally graduated in 1934 and pursued a career in higher education. I met my wife while at Harvard. It was the height of the Great Depression, and she would only agree to marry me if I had a job. So I took the first one I could get. Summing up my life, I would say the best part is that I had a lovely family and an interesting career. I am at work now on my memoirs I want to leave for my sons: it's titled *The Laws of Living.* So far it's quite lengthy."

Louise Brooks—Matriarch

"As the firstborn of five children, I've been working every day since I was seven years old," Louise, 101, often reminds her children, grandchildren, great grandchildren, and great great grandchildren. "My mother and father both worked and I had to stay home taking care of my sick grandmother and my younger brothers and sisters. I would put the dinner on and would have to stand on a box to reach the stove. I never had much of a childhood at all, so I enjoy watching all these kids get started."

Known as a feisty, courageous, energetic woman, "I say what I mean and mean what I say. I'm not afraid to speak my mind if I feel someone is out of line." Her granddaughter, Tonya, adds that she is both deeply loved and widely feared. "She's quick-witted and can still tell you off six ways to Sunday in the blink of an eye."

Louise says she has been blessed not only with long life, but also good health, having never been in a hospital until her mid-90s. "I get around just fine and enjoy reading and doing crossword and number puzzles," she says, "and, of course, keeping an eye on all these kids. On occasion, I still bake biscuits—they all love 'em."

Tonya adds, "Grandma is a matriarch who loves us all with a fierceness that only a mother can. We are proud of her and we love her because as the foundation of our family, the pillar upon which we stand, she has helped make us who we are today."

Helen Haffner, aka "Aunt Honey"

Helen Wright Haffner was born August 12, 1912, in Lapidum, Maryland, where she has lived all her life. Her memory is "clear as a bell," she asserts, and she remembers all the way back to her childhood. One of the stories she likes to tell is when she and her sister were "sky watchers" during WWII, as members of a civilian group called the Ground Observer Corps. They watched with binoculars for German submarines and ships from the Eastern Shore of Maryland. Describing herself as a "true Marylander," she loves steamed crab and is a diehard fan of the Baltimore Orioles. "My favorite color is red."

Most of her married years were spent as a housewife, but when widowed she worked in a vegetable packing house and in a local commercial laundry. A longtime partnership followed, but again, she was left alone. She enjoys playing bingo and cards and belongs to both the local VFW and American Legion.

Helen got her nickname "Aunt Honey" from one of her sister's daughters who when young could not pronounce "Helen," and instead said "Honey." "The name stuck," her niece Debbie says, "because it fit her so well." Described as always a happy and positive person, although she had no children of her own, all of her nieces and nephews and their children are her children and grandchildren, the family tells. For many years, she has been the "reigning matriarch" of the family, all of whom live nearby and visit often, helping with household chores and grocery shopping, so she can maintain the independence she loves.

"In the evening, I enjoy a nip of blackberry brandy, and sometimes a Rolling Rock beer. My grandnephews will stop by and we'll crack one open and have a chat and a good laugh."

Juanita Redpath

"When my husband and I divorced several years ago, I lost him but kept his mother," Nancy begins. "My mother-in-law, Juanita, 101, and I have always been close. Now we live together, travel together, and have a good time. She's an amazing woman. Lately, we've been traveling around the country by car, visiting some of her surviving family members, especially her younger cousins. She enjoys getting together with them and sharing family memories. It's amazing, though, the different perceptions people can have in the same family. Sometimes we'll get in the car to leave and she'll say to me, 'He has that all wrong. That's not what happened.' It's cute," Nancy says. "As the oldest in the family, she's convinced she knows best."

One of Juanita's happiest memories was when she and her five siblings and parents, with all of their belongings, drove in a Model T Ford from Springfield, Illinois, to live in Southern California, camping along the way. "Sometimes we would be lucky and make 100 miles a day," she recalls. "At night we would set up a big canvas tent and cookstove. We kids—the oldest was 14, I was nine—thought it was great fun, but I'm not sure my parents did. When we got to California, relatives who had moved there before us would take one of us in. We were parceled out for a time; sometimes we would live in the tent. It was a few years until my father could build us a home."

"Nita," as she's called, only finished the eighth grade, but says she has never lost her interest in learning. "I was always a reader and loved the library. I like bird books and bird watching, flower books to help with my garden, which I still maintain, and tour guides to read about places I'd like to see. I met my first husband at an open-air dance hall when I was just 16. We married that same year, and our first son was born when I was 17. We had two more children and then divorced. I married my second husband right after the war and we had a son together, the one Nancy was married to. I've seen a lot in my life, from ice deliveries by wagon to the age of electronics, from cod liver oil treatments to heart transplants. It's been a wonderful life."

INTERESTS AND AVOCATIONS

Trudi Fletcher

"Art is my life. I've been involved in art all my life. It is who I am and what I am. I've always tried to be *me*," Trudi says. "In my case, I have always known what I wanted to do, and I am still doing it. Over the course of my career I have done watercolors, oils, silk screens, and batiks. But I think of myself primarily as an artist of watercolors."

True to form, Trudi celebrated approaching her centenary with an art exhibit at the Tubac Center of the Arts, a nonprofit organization in Tubac, Arizona, south of Tucson. It was clear that she was more interested in her lifelong passion of painting than she was in becoming a centenarian, which she dismisses as if to say, "What's age got to do with it?"

"I feel 65," she says. "People have always accepted me as a younger person; why should I tell them my age when I don't feel it? I've always had friends who were younger, sometimes much younger, than I. But now, others think it's a reason to celebrate living 100 years—so I'll be a young 100!

"In fact, my 100th celebration was the first birthday party I've ever had. I was born on Christmas Day, so that is what was always celebrated. But this year my family came from out of state and we went to a nice restaurant for a real birthday party—not a Christmas celebration."

Trudi is a native of Glendale, California, and a graduate of the California College of the Arts and Crafts. She was a high school art teacher during the 1930s, working her way up to department head. "Unlike many of my peers, I was not forced to retire when I married, but I chose to do so when my daughter was on the way in 1941. We moved to New York in 1942 because my husband had a good job offer—he was in finance. Eventually we settled in Ridgewood, New Jersey.

"Robert died in 1958 while my daughter was in college and my son in high school; I remarried four years later. We stayed in New Jersey for a couple of years and then moved to Tucson, Arizona. I enjoyed our frequent trips to Nogales, Arizona, and Mexico. Each time we went, we would drive past the tiny town—an artist's colony, actually—of Tubac, population 200. In 1967 we moved there and I opened an art gallery with my sister, the Dos Hermanas Gallery (the two-sister gallery). I continued to run the gallery until I was 85. While I painted for the joy of it, I liked selling my works, too, and those of others, of course. My gallery was an extension of my interests."

Trudi has found a way to blend her other interest into her art. "I have traveled extensively, studying with great teachers such as Dan Kingman and Millard Sheets, and I studied with The Art Workshop from 1962–2000. I kept on learning. I have taken two around-the-world trips when doing so was a big deal and still unusual. I've also returned to a lot of interesting places several times and have written 50 journals of my trips. It was especially wonderful traveling in the 1960s and 70s when everyone loved Americans, and before everything became westernized. You could go to Bali (I've been twice) and the locals were wearing their native costumes; that's where I learned about Batik; and to Thailand with all its rich raw silk and beautiful colors; and before people in India were wearing jeans. They all look like they're from New York now. I've been to China four times. I loved learning different ways of living and eating and dressing. I loved the native qualities of other cultures. I've been to Africa three times, Nepal twice, India three times.

"Bangkok was a beautiful place; I still have my spirit house in the living room. I've been to the Middle East—to Saudi Arabia and Dubai and Kuwait with my daughter. That was a university trip. I was in Burma when I was 85. That was my last big trip.

"More than anything, my art has been influenced by my travels, by the different cultures, textures, colors of foreign lands. There is always something new to learn. I always felt expanded as a person with each trip. I feel I was directed by my subconscious; everything I have done has been for a reason. This was my way of expressing myself and learning about the world. It is all reflected in my paintings."

Trudi has no intention of putting away her paints and brushes. "I'm working in watercolors again," she says. "My creative spirit remains strong. I'm still evolving. I developed a new style a couple of years ago. I tired of painting landscapes and still life—I began painting people, animals, and birds in a more abstract style—it's been fun. I call my new works *The 98s*, after the age at which I began painting them." It was these Trudi exhibited at her centennial show at the Tubac gallery. The colorful, cheerful works of art are very much a reflection of the bright, attractive artist herself.

Trudi Fletcher

Eleanor Harris

Although vision impaired, Eleanor Harris, 100, was determined to write her stories, as she calls her memoirs, for her sons and family. She began recording what turned out to be 14 tapes with the recorder one of her sons provided. The finished product was a bound book comprising 118 pages including photos of her life over the years.

"I was born in the small town of McCook, Nebraska, on April 4, 1912, at home, as most babies were then. I took up the violin at age 11 and music became my fascination, with music education my major when I attended McCook College. At that time it was only a two-year school. I then went to New York City for two years with a friend who was studying piano. She was 19 and I was 18. We went to the Institute of Musical Art, which was the undergraduate part of the Juilliard School of Music. Then I went back to the University of Nebraska to get my BA. I played in the symphony at the university. I then got a job as a music supervisor in Bayard, Nebraska. My contract stated that if I got married, I was fired. It was the Depression, so we would go along with just about anything.

"Anyway, I saved every cent I could and after two years had enough to move back to New York, where I wanted my life to be. I loved New York, the excitement, the pace, the places to go—the theatre, museums, and concerts—all of it! I went to Columbia and earned a master's degree in music education. I had a grand life planned. I had two cousins who were there also, and we all graduated on the same day. Meanwhile, I had met a young man named John T. Harris, who had recently moved to New York from Alabama. He was really handsome. You can fill in the rest.

"After I graduated, we were married. When John T., Jr. was on the way, my husband said he didn't want to raise a child in New York City, so we moved to Florida and then to

Eleanor Harris

Atlanta, where we had a lot of fun as a young married couple with a baby. We traveled a lot for John T.'s job, and the baby slept in a dresser drawer. We were all very happy. Intermittently, we would make trips back to John T.'s family home in Alabama.

"We moved back to my family home in McCook in 1945, where John T. managed our family department store and cattle ranch and feedlot. By now we had four sons. I had my sixth and last son in 1955 when I was 43, which was old for that time, but everything went well.

"We traveled around so much and it was difficult sometimes with the boys, so John T. decided he would learn to fly because it would be faster. He got his license after the war when he was 44, and flew until he was 70. We would all fit into the plane, a Stinson, with the older boys holding the younger ones on their laps, and the dog in the back on a shelf. That dog loved to fly. When we stopped for gas, it was quite a sight with all of us piling out of the small plane. John T. was very fond of flying, and we had some scary experiences, but we always ended up safely. It's amazing, looking back, the kinds of things people do in their lives. Along the way I got a real estate license, and was on the governor's board to promote business in Nebraska. We traveled to many interesting places in the world—Europe, of course, but also South America, Mexico, China, and Thailand. This was in the 1970s and '80s.

"As the years went on, we started a museum and historical society in McCook; we called it the Museum of the High Plains. At first, we had just my mother's things—she never threw anything out—then it grew into a nice success.

"I also co-founded the McCook Community College Foundation, and was instrumental in starting a community orchestra and chorus, and the implementation of an orchestra in the McCook school system. I continued to play the violin and piano at local events and, of course, at home.

"When we eventually retired to Alabama, John T. wanted to start a museum in his home area also, so we did. After acquiring the building, we put an ad in the newspaper that we were accepting donations, and things began coming in. We expanded to two buildings, put in a garden, and it's a very nice little museum today. We celebrated my 100th birthday there with a reception and party at the Museum of East Alabama, in Opelika.

"It's gratifying to know you have created something that is of value to others."

Margaret Dunning

If you happened to have been at the Concours d'Elegance auto show at Amelia Island, Florida, in March 2013, you surely would have been attracted to the cream-colored 1930 Packard Model 740 Roadster, proudly displayed by its owner Margaret Dunning, of Plymouth, Michigan. The car won two trophies, one for the most popular entry and the other for its artistic beauty, of which Margaret was most pleased; a fitting reward for her loving efforts over the years to restore and maintain the Packard in pristine condition.

Margaret, 102, is the oldest exhibitor, continuing to drive and show her "Beauty," as she named the car she's owned since 1949. Margaret also changes the spark plugs and oil herself, although she leaves the rest to her maintenance team. "For many years I've had a trusted mechanic, who is now in his 90s. Together, we have restored and maintained a number of cars including a 1931 Ford Model A, a 1966 Cadillac Deville, and a 1975 Cadillac Eldorado convertible, all of which I still own and occasionally show at local events in Michigan.

"My father taught me to drive on a Model T Ford when I was eight. I've been in love with cars ever since. He owned a large dairy and potato farm. Henry Ford was our neighbor and a friend of my father's." While other young girls her age were playing with dolls and playing dress up, she says, "I was in the garage tinkering with everything from a tractor to a truck and driving them."

Margaret's early years were affected by two major events: the premature death of her father when she was 12, and later the Great Depression, which began the year she graduated from high school. Forced to drop out after two years at the University of Michigan, she attended the Hamilton Business School in Ypsilanti, while helping at her mother's real estate business. She then worked for a short time making voltage regulators at the Phoenix Mill Ford Plant in Plymouth, a Ford Village Industries plant that employed only women. For the second half of the 1930s, she worked as a bank teller and assistant cashier at a local bank. In the 1940s she worked at the Plymouth United Savings Bank, and for three years during WWII, was a volunteer for the local Red Cross motor pool, driving a truck.

In 1947, Margaret began her business career in earnest. She purchased a clothing store on Main Street in Plymouth and renamed it Dunnings; in 1950, she moved the store to a larger location downtown, and sold it in 1968.

During these years, Margaret's community service in the town of Plymouth began to make an impact. She and her mother donated the building and land to house the local library branch of the county library system. Today it is a central part of the Plymouth library, known as the Dunning-Hough Library. In 1962, Margaret joined the Board of Directors the Community Federal Credit Union in Plymouth, and was president of the board for 19 of the 22 years she served. She clearly had an aptitude for business and under her stewardship the assets of the Credit Union grew from approximately $1 million and one office to $40 million and six offices. The Credit Union established the Margaret Dunning Scholarship Fund in 1989 in honor of her contributions to the Plymouth community.

Margaret's involvement in the community included the Plymouth Historical Society, where, in 1971, she donated the funds to build a new museum to house the community's historical artifacts. In 1998, the museum purchased a sizeable collection of Abraham Lincoln memorabilia. Margaret donated $1 million to expand the museum. She is a permanent member of the board.

In 1997, she established a private grant-making foundation, which bears her name.

Over the years Margaret began collecting, restoring, and showing old cars, continuing her interest that began in her early years. In 1985, she donated a restored 1906 Ford Model N and a 1930 Cadillac convertible to the Gilmore Car Museum in Hickory Corners, Michigan.

Although Margaret has been showing cars for years and belongs to several car clubs, in the past few years she has become a celebrity on the antique car show circuit. But it's not just for show. Margaret is admired for her driving ability and handling of the Packard she exhibits; the 8 cylinder, 4 speed standard transmission car, without power steering. It's a big car, but Margaret handles it with competence. At the 2012 Pebble Beach Concours d'Elegance, where her Packard earned a perfect score, Margaret received a standing ovation from the crowd when presented with the "Belle of the Concourse" trophy at the end of the traditional parade of cars. In order to join the procession, she had to drive up an incline. (To put this in perspective, some of us have difficulty lining up our cars to get them into the tracks of the drive thru car wash, with an automatic shift and power steering. Here's Margaret at 102 with a stick shift and no power steering. Readers who recall driving a car with "four on the floor" will know the skill needed to move precisely using the clutch.) Later, Margaret again demonstrated her driving prowess when navigating up another ramp to the presentation platform, this time to receive an award from the Classic Club of America presented by Jay Leno, who admired both her car and her skill.

Margaret Dunning

"I have a busy schedule in 2013 on the antique car circuit and will show my cars in 12 events around the country. In May I'll be in Seabrook, Texas, at the Keels and Wheels event, one of my favorites. They asked me to show my 1931 Model A Ford. In recognition of Margaret's hands-on approach to maintaining her cars, the FRAM Group, a manufacturer of oil filters and auto parts, awarded her a lifetime supply of their oil, filters, and other products.

Margaret occasionally drives the Packard to local car shows, including the Michigan Region Classic Car Club of America. Her "everyday car" is a 2003 Cadillac Deville.

Summing up her long and happy life, Margaret says, "It's been a good ride, and I am enjoying the opportunities provided by these later years. My favorite quote is an Irish proverb: 'Do not resent growing old, many are denied the privilege.'"

Our centenarians have arrived at the 100-year mark by mastering the art of aging, and most have benefited and will continue to benefit from its science. Part and parcel of their lifestyle choices are the fundamentals of how they have managed their life's work and finances, enabling them to enjoy a good quality of life on their way to 100 and beyond. Now, for the first time, they share with us their wisdom on work and money gained from decades of experience.

CHAPTER 3

Money Wise and Time Tested

HOW THEY THINK WE ARE DOING

SIMPLE SAVING WISDOM: BATTLE OF NEEDS VERSUS WANTS

DEBT IS A FOUR-LETTER WORD

TIME-LY ADVICE

INVESTING TODAY—AFTER A CENTURY OF PERSPECTIVE

DEFINING *RICH*

Over the past 100-plus years, America has experienced numerous economic cycles: hard times and good times, boom times and bust times, and uncertain times. These economic cycles are the inevitable and inescapable fabric everyone in our society wears, and those who live over a century wear it a *lot*.

Most of our centenarians have worn them well.

As our country entered the twentieth century along with the birth of our centenarians, our primarily agricultural society was laying the foundation for an industrial age explosion that would change our country and the entire world forever. World War I began to fuel manufacturing activity that proceeded into the "Roaring Twenties," making for an ecstatic economic expansion in broad areas of our economy including the banking and investment sectors.

An "eat, drink, and be merry for tomorrow we may die" mind-set swept over a lot of our society in the rocking and roaring 1920s as America energetically danced to the Charleston, applauded Wall Street's bullish growth and toasted the country's growing prominence and power in the world. People made fortunes in the stock market, dined generously, and dressed stylishly. In the countryside and cities, Americans were enjoying the postwar good life.

Then, like a rogue tsunami, the Great Depression swept over America like a sledgehammer swatting a housefly. Economically, it brought our great nation to its knees. Unemployment soared to 25 percent, nearly 10,000 banks (almost 40 percent) failed, and the stock market crashed, falling over 87 percent in a brief period of time. Some people did actually jump out of windows in horrific desperation believing all was lost forever. Many people in cities stood in line all day long to receive a mere apple to eat. Gasoline was rationed from city to country. Indeed, it was a depressing time in our nation's short history up to that chapter in its biography.

But, as is often the case, adversity breeds ingenuity and prosperity. With the advent of World War II, like the ancient phoenix, America rose up out of its ashes to become the undisputed industrial and economic leader of the world. Our nation responded to the Pacific and European challenges like a roaring lion, and in leading our allies to victory America surged forward with unprecedented economic expansion and growth.

Throughout the decades following World War II up to 2008, our country has experienced many economic cycles/peaks/valleys/whatever you wish to call them, but fortunately none so dramatic as the Great Depression years.

In 2008 America experienced what most news media consistently described as "the worst economic recession since the Great Depression." Indeed, it was an economic nightmare, with some major investment banks declaring bankruptcy, the Dow Jones Industrial Average dropping 46 percent, unemployment rising to almost 10 percent, and housing values plummeting over 40 percent in a matter of weeks and months. The federal government spent hundreds of billions of dollars to bail out major banks and financial institutions to avoid what most politicians, economists, and media pundits assured us would be another Great Depression.

Today, as *Celebrate 100* goes to press, our country is still in what we would consider uncertain economic times. Depending on with whom you discuss this topic, we are either slowly recovering, still in the valley, or just really don't know the true status of our economy.

But one thing about your future is very certain: there will continue to be economic peaks and valleys in your lifetime, some more dramatic than others, and travel through them you must. And you need all the wisdom and advice and assistance you can get for the journey.

Having a little better understanding and appreciation for what our class of centenarians have economically endured and survived these past 100-plus years and are still taking in stride, perhaps you will listen intently to their wisdom, advice, and "secrets" on how to more successfully navigate our world of money, finance, and economics.

They are not perfect. They have made mistakes. You may or may not like any or all of their advice. You may think some of their actions and advice are wise, and you may be convinced that some of it is outdated and not relevant to our current state of the economy. You may choose to not practice/implement a single secret suggestion or you may choose to incorporate them all in your everyday financial decisions.

But here is a question we hope you will consider as you explore this chapter. How will implementing some or all of these financial-related decisions impact my stress level in life? Please keep that question in mind as you journey through the next several pages.

We believe it is one key to unlock some of our centenarians' secrets for your success in business and life, no matter what your current age or financial position today.

HOW THEY THINK WE ARE DOING

One of the first questions we asked our centenarians was "How well do you think the younger generation (that's you!) is managing its money?"

In his classic poem "To a Louse," Robert Burns penned these words after observing a very haughty woman parading into the front pew of a church service, purposefully late so everyone could admire all her regalia, dressed to the nines thinking very highly of herself, yet unaware of a filthy louse crawling out from within her piled up hairdo and up the back of her scalp. While she was thinking so highly of herself, Burns and others could not think of anything except how filthy and dirty her hair must be underneath all the external pile of ribbons and bows.

> *Oh would the power some gift He give us, to see ourselves as others see us, It would from many a blunder free us.*

Our centenarians have seen and observed their children and grandchildren—in some cases great grandchildren—managing or mismanaging money and finances through every economic cycle over the past century. We wanted to hear their compliments, critiques, thoughts, and perspectives from their century-plus vantage point. What "grade" would they give us? Whether or not we agreed with their assessment, we thought it wise to listen and consider. It might from many a blunder free us lest we think more highly of ourselves than we ought!

In response to our question, the following are representative quotes and observations from the majority of our seasoned observers.

Rachel Lehmann, 102, is one of our feisty, full-of-life, and very opinionated centenarians who is more active than most people 30 years her junior. She can read a phone book without any glasses, volunteers at the Atlanta Ballet organization on a weekly basis, and still does a little dancing with her 80-something "young" friend. She told us that "where we grew up there were six houses and one cow. Each home owned the cow!" When we posed our question to Rachel, she emphatically replied, "They're so in debt. And why? Because I must have a better TV than you have. Or I must have this new one. Or that new one. All these things they *must* have . . . it's not necessary."

Lucille Burkhardt

—————— ✎◯◯◯◯ ——————

Lula Johnston, 100, astutely observed: "A lot of
young people today very quickly get in over
their heads. It's not good."

Lucille Burkhardt, 100, really became passionate about her response. "For one thing, they've never been through a depression. They don't have any idea what it means. They think they do. They don't. They don't know what it means to watch men stand in a line to get an apple to eat. They don't know what it means for people to practically beg for something to eat for their families. They can't even conceive of it. They're not managing it (money) at all. Everything that goes out goes on their credit card. I don't know what they're gonna do when some of them are forced to pay when times get really bad."

—————— ✎◯◯◯◯ ——————

Julia Buxton carefully observed: "They're spending it too fast.
As fast as they make it."

Our prince of positive thinking, Daniel Merlini, energetically
commented: "They've lost their way. They don't know
where the heck they're going."

Entrepreneur and southern steel magnolia Lillian Cox, 104,
insightfully suggested: "They have two or three credit
cards and charged to the limit. It's very bad."

Clara Wortman

The oldest known Red Hatter in the United States, Ethel Barnhart, 101, somberly concluded: "They don't know the value of money. They need to be taught more about it."

Our sweet Clara Wortman, 106, who was born in Germany and came to the States when she was young, had an interesting perspective: "People want too much. They are not happy with anything. They've had too much since they were small. And, of course, it keeps on and on and they want more and more and it has no end." Clara continued to talk about what she considered to be the definition of *rich,* which she wishes young people would embrace earlier in life because they seem to be wearing themselves out to get financially rich. "Rich is to be alive, be healthy, and have the Lord on your side. Every day He gives me strength and courage for living. And that is important to me. Otherwise, money doesn't mean anything. It's nice when you have it, but I'm just fine if I have enough of what I need." When asked what she would do if we could give her a million dollars, she instantly replied with a laugh, "I'd give it away!"

Loren Cartwright, 100, an energetic and thoughtful "young" centenarian offered up this assessment: "They have no idea what they're gonna hit when it comes to retirement. It comes up to retirement and they don't have anything. They're still in debt. They're still working hard. What are they gonna do? I feel sorry for these people."

Jesse Ward, 100, had a balanced response to our question: "Some of them are blowing it away. Some of them are learning."

The bottom line from most of our centenarians is that the younger generation has not done very well. At least not nearly as well as they could or should have, given the abundance of wealth and opportunity that has passed before them. They believe we have borrowed too much; spent too much; been too impatient, with a "must have it now" mentality; not saved enough; and are living beyond our means too much and too long. From their century of perspective we have a lot of room for improvement.

Many of them acknowledged that they also could have done a much better job managing finances, but most of them have not experienced the levels of personal debt, conspicuous consumption, and financial stress that characterize a large percentage of today's population. You might consider some of their observations and be freed from some blunders going forward.

Certainly, no one wants to live 100-plus years with financial stress and worry most of the time. The majority of our centenarians practiced simple yet what we believe to be profound financial principles that are some of the secrets to their enjoying life long and strong.

SIMPLE SAVING WISDOM: BATTLE OF NEEDS VERSUS WANTS

In the 1950s America was what we label a saving nation. The annual savings rate reached as high as 12 percent during our expanding industrial growth following WWII, and parents of Baby Boomers were economy minded and frugal. Starting in the 1960s the savings rate began to precipitously drop such that by 2005 it had dipped to below 2 percent. It has crept back up to somewhere around 4 to 5 percent, depending on whose statistics you wish to believe.

A plethora of "wow statistics" abounds from numerous sources, suggesting that most Americans have saved only about $50,000 by retirement age; that most Americans are technically bankrupt, meaning that if they had to liquidate everything they own today, they would owe more than they own; and that many if not most people will probably have to stay in the workforce much longer than anticipated (not necessarily a bad thing—read the next chapter) while experiencing a retirement standard of living substantially less than hoped for as they began their working careers.

Saving money—or spending it—is for most people a battle between needs and wants. The gist of our psychological financial battle is deciding what we will spend or save on a need or a want. You need food to survive. You can get by on a $5 sandwich and soda to sustain your physical well-being for several hours. But you may want a fabulous $50 lunch at your favorite fancy Italian restaurant. If you have enough money for either and opt for the sandwich, you saved $45. If you choose the $50 fancy fare, you decided to spend for your want, that is, *not save* $45. Pretty simple. The same principle applies for cars, clothes, homes, appliances, furniture, everything.

Just like you, our centenarians have been engaging in the battle of needs versus wants—spending versus saving—for over 100 years. Recognizing this dynamic in their lives just like ours, we asked them specifically this question:

"What percentage of a person's annual income should they *try* to save—no matter how much or how little they make?"

We were not looking just for what they actually *did* during their vast expanse of life. Some of their advice is "do as I say, not as I did." Many of them recognized that they learned from their mistakes and failure to practice certain sound principles earlier in life.

As Samuel Jones, 101, thoughtfully pointed out, "At age 14 I got paid every 2 weeks and started the bad habit of borrowing from loan sharks on the off week, and then had to pay them off the next week, and then was broke again. I did finally learn to save my money."

So they certainly are not perfect, but we can learn and live a lot more wisely by heeding their successes, failures, and advice based on a century-plus of doing "battle" with wants and needs, saving and spending.

The vast majority—over 90 percent—strongly suggested that 10 percent is the absolute minimum you should try and save each year to prepare for your future, no matter how long you live. Many of them did save that much (or more) throughout their lives, but many confessed that they did not achieve that benchmark but wished they had, and if they had their lives to live over again would certainly achieve that minimum percentage and more.

Ruth Proskaur Smith, 101, emphatically offered: "Try to save
10 percent at least."

Bill Hartkopf, 100, exclaimed, "Save 10 percent. Don't be a gambler!"

Julia Buxton thoughtfully replied, "Save 10 percent.
That is a small amount, but it is a start."

Surprisingly, however, almost a third of our Centenarians energetically exhorted us that you should save a minimum of 20, 30, even 50 percent of your income! Over and over again we heard the phrase pointedly exclaimed, "It's not what you make, it's what you decide to spend!" In essence, you can save 10 percent or more at any income level, as absurd as that may seem to many people today. For that section of our centenarian "class," they have either won the battle of needs over wants, or they are wise enough to encourage us that we had better win it or suffer the ambiguous and perhaps uncomfortable consequences of our future financial challenges.

Maxine Garranson, a tough-skinned, soft-hearted, and full of vim and vigor centenarian from Texas just grinned from ear to ear and informed us, "I learned at an early age just how extravagant my mother was. So, instead, I started saving. You should save at least a third of your income." And she has.

When we asked our feisty Rachel Lehmann, 101, this savings question, she immediately responded, "*All* of it!" Startled, we suggested to Rachel that you cannot save all of your income. You must spend some of it on basic needs—food, clothing, and shelter—for survival. Her witty reply was: "You asked me how much someone should *try* and save. You should *try* and save *all* of it. But, if you make a dollar, you put 50 cents in the bank!"

We inquired, "Fifty percent? Did you do that during your lifetime?"

"Absolutely."

Bottom line on saving secret: our wise, insightful, thoughtful, and experienced centenarians suggest 10 percent as an absolute minimum. Almost a third suggest 20 to 50 percent.

America is somewhere around 4 to 5 percent.

How are you doing? How should you be doing?

Rachel Lehman

DEBT IS A FOUR-LETTER WORD

There are many "four letter words" in today's vocabulary that have very negative if not obscene connotations and, if uttered in certain public venues, can get you in a lot of trouble. If shouted to the wrong party, they can get you seriously injured, if not killed.

Unfortunately for most of our society today, *debt* does not appear to be one of those obscene words that people believe can seriously injure or perhaps even kill them. But most centenarians believe it should be.

We asked our centenarians about debt. We asked them to reflect on the 100-plus years of living and share their thoughts, insights, counsel, advice, and wisdom about managing debt and its impact on quality and quantity of life.

Sadly, they believe debt has become a normal way of life for tens of millions of Americans, and even worse for our local, state, and federal governments. They are right in their assessment. As *Celebrate 100* is published, the U.S. household consumer debt profile is sobering: Average credit card debt is over $15,000; average mortgage debt is almost $150,000; and average student loan debt is just short of $35,000. In total, consumers have accumulated over $11 trillion in debt, almost $850 billion in credit card debt and close to $1 trillion in student loan debt. Over 60 percent of Americans in debt spend one to three hours a day worrying about money, and over 20 percent spend four or more hours worrying. This four-letter word is harming a lot of people.

Essentially, most of our centenarians hate debt. And that is not too strong a word for their feelings about this financial four-letter word.

There is not enough room in this chapter to articulate all the responses and advice we received about debt. The following are just a few that represent the hundreds of nuggets of wisdom and insightful advice.

――――――― ເ໐໐ວ ―――――――

Ellis Joel Daniel, 101, told us: "I never went into debt and owed the bank. I just never did."

Emma Victoria Johnson, 102, exclaimed, "Don't get into debt whatever you do!"

"Don't go into debt—it is too expensive," John Donnelly, 100, astutely observed.

"Debt makes a slave of you," retorted Nicholos Dubovy, 100.

Harry Steine, 100, wisely commented: "Stay out of debt.
Being in debt can make you unhappy."

Garnett Cobb, one of the most energetic and optimistic centenarians that we
encountered, observed: "A lot of people are in debt over their head. Don't buy
anything unless you can pay for it in cash."

We hope you get a "sense" of their feelings, emotions, and suggestions about debt.
In rapid fire we asked the following six questions to summarize our inquiry about their
use of and advice about debt:

1. Did you ever go in debt to buy clothing or jewelry? Almost 100 percent said *no.*
2. Did you ever go in debt to buy a TV, radio, boom box, or stereo system?
   Almost 100 percent said *no.*
3. Did you ever go in debt to take a vacation or luxury trip? Almost 100
   percent said *no.*
4. Did you ever go in debt to buy an automobile? Almost 100 percent said *no.*
5. Did you ever go in debt to buy food or eat out at restaurants? Almost 100
   percent said *no.*
6. Did you ever go in debt to buy furniture for your home? Almost 100
   percent said no.

Many of our centenarians believe that we, the younger generation, are obsessed
with debt because we are allowing wants to win over needs. Their advice is pretty clear
regarding debt: conquer it.

TIME-LY ADVICE

Overwhelmingly, the American way of life has evolved to most people paying for many
goods and services "over time"—installment purchases, minimum monthly payment plans, and so on. Many of us purchase cars, homes, clothing, furniture, jewelry,

televisions, sound systems, electronic gadgets, vacations, and even food "over time" with the use of credit cards and convenient long-term installment payment plans.

We asked our centenarians to share their experiences, perspectives, and advice about buying things over time. Certainly, they all have had a *lot* of time to shop till they drop!

Cash for Cars: *Not* a Government Program

If we are brutally honest with ourselves, purchasing an automobile is not a needs decision. It is not an "obtain reliable and safe means of transportation" decision. It is an emotional wants decision. It is an "I wanna/gotta have it" decision.

And that is OK.

But shiny colors, the smell of new leather, spine-tingling sound systems, and intriguing electronic gadgetry are intoxicating. They combine to encourage many of us to stretch beyond our affordable needs capacity into unaffordable—or uncomfortable—wants decisions by means of easy monthly payments for eternity.

Over 70 percent of all cars in America are purchased on some type of payment plan over time. About 18 percent of our population leases their automobiles, and only 12 percent pay all cash at purchase.

We asked our centenarians: How did you pay for your first car? How have you purchased cars throughout your life?

Over 80 percent paid cash for their first and subsequent car purchases during their 100-plus years of living, and in many cases 80-plus years of driving!

Many of them exclaimed that often they would have liked a bigger, fancier, and more expensive luxurious automobile. And many if not most could have done so if they had decided to finance the car and pay for it "over time." But they didn't. They exercised the discipline of need over want. They did battle and they won. They just did not want the stress of debt and did not want to be a slave to a lender. Not a right-or-wrong decision. Just a freedom-from-stress one.

"I saved my money and paid cash for it," says Ann White, 100.

Loren Cartwright, 100, proudly proclaimed: "So I saved my money, and when I got $40 I bought my first car."

Robert Martin, 100, pointed out that "I bought lots of cars over my lifetime and I always paid cash."

We loved the response given us by Fermin Montes de Oca, more fondly known as Mr. D, 104: "You could buy a Model T for $5. That was the best car Ford ever made." He paid cash.

Dewey Wilson

There were a small percentage who either chose or just had to finance their first and/or subsequent auto purchases. But most of them had the same attitude toward debt as has been previously described and is captured in our "Still Driving at 100" Reverend Dewey Wilson, 100, asserts: "If I could make two payments, I'd make two payments in one month." He did not like the stress or cost of debt and paid off loans ahead of schedule and as quickly as possible. "Let's you and me go drive," he said with a grin. "Just got my license renewed and I drive almost every day. I haven't gotten a ticket in the last 15 years. I used to get tickets, but I know how to drive now!" We jumped in and he toured us all around Lakeland, proudly pointing out landmarks he has enjoyed for a century.

Cars are enticing. And they also were/are to our centenarians. Take their advice or pay the price over time: Pay cash for cars.

House of Cards

Using credit cards is not a good-or-bad, right-or-wrong decision. It's how you use them that positively or negatively impacts your life and stress level. In 2012 the average household credit card debt was over $15,000. Over 4 percent of cardholders were 60 days late on monthly payments. Over 15 percent have been late at least once in making a payment, and 8 percent have entirely missed a monthly payment. Over 54 percent regularly pay only the minimum monthly required amount and only 30 percent regularly pay off the entire amount owed at the end of each month. Many of our centenarians have never used a credit card. They have simply paid cash for everything. But lots of our centenarians have and still use credit cards for convenience and record keeping.

However, overwhelmingly, 90-plus percent of them pay off their credit card balance in full every single month. They cannot stand the pain of carrying forward a balance and paying high interest. To them, it just does not make sense to do so.

Frances Zisso, 101, a lovely, energetic, straight-shooter centenarian in Florida shared with us that "I don't believe in credit cards. You have your money; go out and buy it and forget about it. Why do you want a credit card?!"

Robert Martin, 100, echoed Frances by noting, "Never used a credit card. I didn't want to pay interest. I wanted to keep it for myself."

Lucille Burkhart joined the chorus: "Credit cards. They should be done away with. I don't like them."

And our world's oldest man, Walter Breuning, 114, who has a strong opinion on everything, chimed in: "Never had one, never used one. Tear them up."

But Jack Borden, 101, our world's oldest practicing attorney, represented a respectable percentage of centenarians who use credit cards by intelligently suggesting, "I have credit cards now. But I'm the type they don't like. I pay it off right away."

Their loud, overwhelming, unified chorus of advice to us is: You will be better off not to use them. They can get you in trouble. But if you use credit cards, pay them off in full every single month. On time. Never pay penalty or interest expense. Not only is that unwise, it is stupid. Their words, not ours.

Castles or Coffins?

The phrase "A man's home is his castle" has been bantered around for over a century. For men and women alike, owning a home has become one of the key elements to living the American Dream.

Millions of Americans have shared in this wonderful component that characterizes our nation as one of hope and prosperity and opportunity. But in recent years, for many, the American Dream has morphed into the American Nightmare, causing untold stress, sadness, and despair coupled with massive financial loss.

Many economic, financial, and, of course, political experts purport that the subprime mortgage crisis was the primary factor contributing to what has been journalistically headlined as the worse economic recession since the Great Depression. Simply stated, people borrowed more money than they could afford to purchase more home than they could afford (wants won the battle over needs). When they could no longer meet their mortgage payment obligation, their "castle" became a "coffin," burying them in debt.

There were over two million homeowner foreclosures in 2012 with even more projected for 2013. Over 5 percent of homeowners were at least two months late on their mortgage payments in 2012.

Our centenarians' wisdom and advice about buying a house is simple and straightforward. Wait to buy what you can comfortably afford. The majority of them saved at least 20 percent for a down payment, and many saved and put down even more. Their monthly payments were comfortably affordable, not stressful. They balanced need with want successfully.

As we walked around his property, we asked Mr. Porter Edwards how he purchased his farm, truck, tractor (both of which he still drives at 104). He stopped dead in his tracks and asked, "What do you mean?" We inquired if he had borrowed money to purchase his equipment or had a mortgage on his farm, where he still plows and grows a lovely garden annually.

He looked us straight in the eye and slowly said, "If I didn't have the cash to pay for it, I didn't buy it." With that he turned around and continued the tour of his picturesque

Porter Edwards

South Georgia 40-acre farm—all paid for in cash as he earned it from planting and picking many different kinds of crops over 100 years.

Contrarian Consideration

We would be incomplete in our reporting if we did not mention Walter Breuning, the world's oldest man according to the *Guinness Book of World Records*. Walter was a contrarian in that he was a renter most of his life. He purchased a house at a young age, but lived in it just a few years. He described that owning a house "was just too much trouble to keep it up. I never did like yard work." He sold it and has rented the rest of his life.

So it is worth noting that the world's oldest man did not have the worry of a mortgage, yard work, and house maintenance. And he certainly experienced his share of the American Dream. Something to think about and consider.

INVESTING TODAY—AFTER A CENTURY OF PERSPECTIVE

When it comes to financial products, services, and investment opportunities—both good and bad—our centenarians have seen it all over the last 100-plus years. With this amazing long-term perspective and panoramic context, we wanted to capture their wisdom and advice about this important aspect of our lives. We asked them the question: "Where do you believe is the best place to invest money today?"

We invited them to think about the many decades of their adult years, all the financial investment products they have read about, heard about, seen on television, observed others experiencing, or have personally experienced themselves.

Perhaps hoping for an overwhelming majority centenarian investment wisdom nugget that would encourage us to pour all our money into, we were impressed with their wise, commonsense, and thoughtful perspectives, suggestions, and advice.

Les Oldt is one of the most active, energetic, articulate, and astute centenarians we have encountered. At 107 he still goes flying with his son a couple of times monthly;

bakes delicious breads, which we have enjoyed; and barbecues some mean ribs. He still uses a typewriter (remember what that is?) and sends us frequent notes, suggestions, recipes, and articles to keep us informed on interesting and helpful subjects. He is an intelligent, knowledgeable investor who keeps up with all the financial news, collaborating regularly with his son Tom, who is a financial adviser.

When we asked Les the investing question, he requested some time to think about a response. A few days later we received the insightful and instructive poem "Investing Today," which we believe captures most of the distilled essence of the combined responses from our 500-plus centenarians. (See page 92.)

What is the bottom line of Les's poetic wisdom? Diversify.

As Les wisely pointed out to us in one of our conversations, no one ever invests in a bad deal. We never enthusiastically knowingly direct our money into a wonderful bad deal. We all invest in some good deals that go bad. Gains and losses are inevitable over a lifetime of investing, and certainly over a century.

Les Oldt

He thoughtfully articulates from a 100-plus years of experience that "eventually good times will prevail" (e.g., economic cycles are inevitable), "if one chooses to be too pessimistic, he is most likely to fail" (e.g., don't sit on the sideline or stuff your money in a mattress—proactively invest with diversity), and "no one can make that magic call" (e.g., get good advice to help you diversify your investments into several asset classes—don't put all your eggs in one basket).

The collective wisdom, advice, and responses from our centenarians represented the entire investment kaleidoscope articulated in Les's instructive poem. Investing in your own business, certificates of deposit (CDs), T-bills, stocks, bonds, mutual funds, real estate, exchange-traded funds (ETFs), gold and silver and precious metals, insurance, and of course the best one of all: your health.

There was no "silver bullet" overwhelming majority response. No single asset class was the clear-cut centenarian champion for you to pour most or all of your money into and expect perpetual financial abundance. Their answers were as diversified as Les's poetic wisdom.

INVESTING TODAY

How best to invest today you ask-
Finding an answer is a difficult task

The task seemed qjite easy in former years-
And you did the job without shedding tears.

And it seems most investor advisors could be trusted-
But today,if you follow some, you are apt to get busted.

So today, it seems best to put on your thinking cap-
Or just settle down for a long winter nap.

For many years past, the choice was cow pastures and farms
That is if you didn't mind getting sub burned arms.

Then manypfarmers gave up on their crops-
and moved into town and opened up a small shop.

And then corporations. big and strong
Offered their stocks and bonds to the throngs.

Finally, vast mutual funds came to stay
And thousands of investors headed their way.

More recently, ETF's came to the fore-

And offered investors morecash than before.

Mortgages for many years offereda goodly feast-
Then came sub-prime, that awful beast.

Cd's and T Bills gave some peace-
Then intterest on them came almost to cease.

So now we seek something different and bold-
And our thoughts turn quite naturally to gold.

Or is silver perhaps the real thing to own-
Or may it too cause us to moan ?

Chances are that eventually good times will prevail
So, if one chooses to be too pessimistic, he is most likely to fail.

It appears no one has a crystal ball-
No one can make that magic call.

So why not be most thankful for Vibrant good health-
Which after all is the very best form of wealth ?

March 11, 2009   L.M.O.

Kathryn Dwinnell, 107, our very first interview for this project, whose son Dick is also a financial adviser, pointed out that the concept and principle of diversification is not new. Over 3,000 years ago King Solomon, purportedly the wisest and richest man that ever lived, instructed his people, "Divide your shares into seven or eight—for you do not know what disaster will come upon the land." Translation in today's language and context: Over a long period of time, certainly a century, every asset class may experience some "disaster" of some magnitude. So "divide your shares"—diversify your investments—and you have a greater probability of faring well over your financial journey.

Andy Weinandy, 100, expressed his conviction that one of the best investments you can make is employing a competent, trustworthy financial adviser to assist you in prudent planning and investment.

"I think if you have any money that you're going to invest at all, you ought to have a financial adviser. Otherwise, it's just like taking a dart and putting a financial page of the paper on the wall and throwing it at the paper and picking stocks by the dart way of picking. That isn't the way."

Best and Worst Financial Decisions

If you live 100-plus years, your hundreds if not thousands of financial decisions will shape and determine the quality, character, content, and enjoyment of your life journey. Being mortal, you will definitely score in all three decision-making categories: Good, Bad, and Ugly. And centenarians have experienced their fair share of all three.

As we listened to them think out loud and share their thoughts and advice on where they believe are the best places to invest money today based on their extremely long-term perspective and knowledge continuum, we also wanted to know what they perceived to be their best (Good) and worst (Bad-Ugly) financial decisions. We were hoping that their "case studies" might be instructive to us for maximizing our best/Good scores and minimizing our worst/Bad-Ugly scores. We asked these two questions:

1. What is the *best* financial decision you ever made?
2. What is the *worst* financial decision you ever made?

Like the responses to our investing question, we received a rainbow of answers, all of which contained solid content from which we can learn and benefit.

The *best* decision answers ran the gamut of diversity with no clear major majority.

Louis Reitz, 100, made a habit of "investing in what appears to be a safe company."

Our youthful world's oldest water skier, Dr. Frank Shearer, 105, told us, "Most of the money I have made outside of working was in mutual funds."

Garnett Beckmann, 101, enjoyed success with stock and bond investing and proudly informed us: "As fast as those dividends came in, I poured them right back into the company. I was getting along without them and every dividend that came I made it into a check and let it go right back."

Richard John Morris, 102, offered: "I had the conviction that real estate was always something that was going to be needed."

One of our centenarians, whom we shall allow to remain anonymous, gleefully exclaimed, "Marrying my second husband!" She joyfully recounted the many tangible and intangible dividends from this strategic investment decision.

The "Twinkle" Factor

The best/Good financial decisions covered the entire spectrum of financial diversification: stocks, bonds, mutual funds, real estate, insurance, savings accounts, precious metals, and starting their own business. But there was one answer frequently given that caused a "twinkle in their eyes"—what we fondly labeled the Twinkle Factor.

"When we bought our house."
Sue Royal, 100

"Buying my house."
Teddy (Theresa) Shallow, 102

"We bought the farm."
Emma Johnson, 102

Carl Azar

The words varied from person to person, but the meanings were identical. Buying their house or farm, or paying off the mortgage and owning it free and clear brought a psychological, celebratory "return on investment" that was freeing, satisfying, and even exhilarating for most. We saw the twinkle in their eyes as they described the various paths to owning their homes, which included years of hard work, saving, sacrificing, being frugal, resisting temptations to splurge and give in to emotional wants, and keeping their eyes focused on the goal of debt-free home ownership.

The Good financial decision responses far outweighed the worst financial decision answers. The vast majority of surveys left this answer blank, and in the personal interviews there were often long periods of silence when asked about their worst financial decision.

Carl Azar, 100, was born in Lebanon and moved to America in his mid-20s. He was a master furniture craftsman and worked robustly until retiring at age 97. He drove until he was 95. At his 100th birthday party we enjoyed seeing Carl honored with warm wishes, decorations galore, food fit for a king, and a magnificent birthday cake. When asked what is the best thing about being 100, he gladly replied, "Bringing my family and friends together." Carl never dreamed he would live to be 100 and did not even think about that notion until he turned 99. "Big Daddy," as his family calls him, told us the key to a great long life is to "keep good, keep busy, and keep thinking about tomorrow." When asked about his financial successes and failures from which he has learned, he finally confessed, "I traded several cars before they were worn out." That was about the worst financial decision he could remember.

Lillian Cox

Believe it or not, another anonymous centenarian exclaimed that her worst financial decision was marrying her second husband! Sometimes you win. Sometimes you lose.

But the most profound answer to this question is one we hope you will pay very close attention to in the following paragraphs. We believe it is one of the most important secrets and nuggets of wisdom that we can share with you for a full and celebratory life, no matter how long you live.

Don't Bet on *Not* Living to 100!

Lillian Cox, 104, is a stunningly beautiful, red-blooded, true-blue American entrepreneur. Everything about her just beams with beauty and charm and grace. She invited us to her lovely home where she lives and enjoys gardening almost daily. When asked what her best financial decision in life was, without hesitation she said, "Starting my own business. I opened an elegant ladies' boutique shop here in Tallahassee in my early 30s. The store was very successful and I made lots of money."

Smiling the entire time, she enthusiastically told us how much she enjoyed building the business, making many friends, and having the fun and satisfaction of dressing Tallahassee's finest. Indeed, it was her best imaginable financial and life decision.

She continued telling us that her father died at 35, her mother died at 64, and her oldest sister had passed away at the ripe old age of 71. "So I just figured that I would live to be about 70 at the most."

"When I turned 65, I made the worst financial decision of my life. I decided to sell my store, since I figured I had only a few more years to live. So I made a lot more money when I sold it and decided to travel all over the world with my family and friends. And I did. You name it, I've been there!"

So over the next five years Lillian traveled the globe in style, enjoying the fruits of her successful business career, and as she says somewhat tongue-in-cheek with a charming sense of humor, "I spent all my money! I didn't die, and now I've been broke for over 30 years!"

Lillian never dreamed she would live to be 100. It never crossed her mind. She went on to articulate that had she known she was going to live so long, she would have made a few different financial decisions and plans when she was 65. Maybe she would have gone economy class a couple of times or taken not quite as many friends and relatives with her on those exotic trips!

Here is the bottom-line, golden nugget secret you should take away from Ms. Lillian: don't bet on *not* living to be 100. None of us know if we will live to be 100. Of the 500-plus centenarians we have studied, less than 10 thought they would make it to 100 and longer. But they did. And many of you will also. Even if you think you won't.

Therefore, plan on it. Plan for it. Get whatever advice and counsel and encouragement you can from this book and other resources to leverage your "bet" on making it to 100. Do everything possible to develop a sound financial plan and strategy to maximize your probability of comfortably coasting to the centenarian finish line and beyond. If you do, you are golden. If you check out a little early, your heirs will appropriately mourn and then gratefully celebrate your wisdom, financial acumen, and premature generosity.

DEFINING *RICH*

Various studies by financial firms have asked people how much money they need to have to consider themselves rich. Answers range from thousands to hundreds of millions of dollars. In one survey people defined *rich* as someone whose net worth was roughly double theirs—whether they were worth thousands or millions.

Our centenarians represent all socioeconomic levels from across our country. We purposefully asked the question "How do you define the word *rich?*" in the middle of our questioning them about money and financial matters. Our desire was to determine if they would respond in some financial terms or definitions, or something else that was shaped from a century of experiences.

Sophie Birk, 100, still lives in her home and still drives. "They don't want me driving. My grandson says, 'Look out pedestrians, here comes Sophie!'" She is quick to point out, "There's nothing wrong with my mind. Age to me doesn't mean anything. Age is just a number. And a birthday party. That's about it." When asked what is the greatest thing about turning 100, she laughingly replied, "We had about 10 birthday parties. Those parties kind of do you in, you know."

Sophie Birk

Sophie is one of the toughest, most tenacious, and most positive centenarians we had the joy of meeting. "I've had quite a few surgeries. Two spinal fusions, three hip replacements, knee surgery, and a lot of other things," she says with a smile and laughter.

She is an astute investor who received wise counsel from her father from a very young age. "My father said if I got a nickel I had to put a penny in the bank. And I did. And I saved money all the time I was a little kid. Then in 1929, when the crash came, I had money. But nobody else did. There were people jumping out of windows because they lost their shirt. It was horrible. It was terrible." Because of her disciplined saving from youth, Sophie was not negatively impacted by the Depression. "Didn't bother me at all. Because I could go with the tide. I've never borrowed money. If I didn't have the money, I didn't buy it."

She even did the unimaginable in today's world of easy credit and friendly home mortgages. "I paid cash for the house—$10,000. I invested in a little bit of everything. Bought a house and sold it. Bought property and sold it. Mostly put my money on mortgages and made sure they could pay me back." Her secret to living 100 happy, healthy, optimistic years? "I just was happy. My dad would say eat, sleep, and run. Love yourself. Have faith in yourself, and you'll never have anything to worry about. Oh yeah, I kind of like myself!" she gleefully retorts with her winsome laughter and smile.

When we asked Sophie to define the word *rich,* she didn't hesitate a moment. "You can be poor and still feel rich. Rich is a state of mind." A wise piece of advice from an energetic centenarian who told us in response to our comment that we would just love to hang out with her, "I don't think you could keep up with me!" And we probably couldn't.

Although we did receive a few financially oriented answers, most of the hundreds of responses were not monetary in nature, reminiscent of Sophie's definition. We close this chapter with a few representative centenarian definitions of *rich* that are helpful, enlightening, instructive, inspiring, and encouraging for us all.

"The richest thing is to have a good family life."
LEORA JESTERS, 105

"To make a good living and put something in the bank."
Bertha Wolfe, 100

"Comfortable—money isn't everything."
Elvira Renschler, 101

*"A poor person money-wise often has a treasury full of
friends and experiences."*
Irene Packard, 101

"Being loved."
Kathryn Dwinnell, 107

"The things that are really rich in your life are the things that you love."
Elois Morris Wright, 100

*"You always heard it said that a man who has one friend is worth a
million dollars. I tell people that if that's the way we're measured,
I'm worth more than the entire debt of the United States because
I have a lot of friends."*
Jack Borden, 101, world's oldest practicing attorney

*"Rich is when you've got food for your family and you've got
clothes for your family and you can support them in good shape."*
Walter Breuning, 114, world's oldest man

*"I think if you have a loving family and all, you're richer
than anything money can buy."*
Ethel Barnhart, 100

"I don't care about being a millionaire. I'm a millionaire now. I'm healthy; I'm sitting here talking with you. I know what I'm talking about and I'm healthy."
BERNANDO LaPOLLA, 107

"A rich person is one with a lot of spirit and zest for life and who enjoys people and helps them, too."
MARIANNE CROWDER, 103, WORLD'S OLDEST GIRL SCOUT

"Oh gee, you can be rich in lots of ways. You don't have to have money to be rich. If you've got a wonderful family that you love and that love you, then you're rich."
LOREN CARTWRIGHT, 100

"Rich in love, rich with friends, rich in your work, rich with family—that is what I call rich."
CARLOS MUSSENDEN, 100

"Enjoying life is rich. I'm rich."
ROBERT MARTIN, 100

Lessie Smithgall, 100

We collected hundreds more definitions of *rich* from these special people who have over a century of life perspective. Money can certainly be part of the definition, but, as you can see, they view rich as so much more than financial reward and security.

A final piece of wisdom and advice from one of our centenarians. Write down your definition of rich on a piece of paper. Think about it and be specific rather than using vague and "wandering generality" language. Then start doing and being whatever you must to achieve and live your personal definition of rich.

Whether you live to be 100 or not, your life will be richer in every way—like it has been and continues to be for our very wise and rich centenarians.

CHAPTER 4

Work Wisdom

TAKE THIS JOB AND LOVE IT

FROM SUCCESS TO SIGNIFICANCE

TEACHERS EXTRAORDINAIRE

KEEPING UP AND KEEPING ON

WISE WORK ADVICE

As many of our centenarians were being born, President Theodore Roosevelt robustly contended that no person in America ever needed to be pitied because "far and away, the best prize that life has to offer is the chance to work hard at work worth doing."

Unless you happen to be born with a silver, gold, or platinum spoon in your mouth, you will spend close to half of your waking hours for a large part of your adult life working at something. There is a proliferation of work/job satisfaction surveys conducted by numerous educational, governmental, and research organizations annually, and the results vary as much as the estimates on exact population numbers of centenarians in our country. Some show that over 80 percent of Americans hate their jobs, while others indicate that the vast majority of Americans love what they do. Go figure.

As most of our centenarians described their work, it reminded us of the story about three different stonemasons performing their craft. When a young boy stopped by the first stone worker and asked what he was doing, the stonemason frustratingly exclaimed, "I'm trying to cut this stone and it's breaking my back." The boy quickly moved on and passed by another worker who did not appear to be so languished and asked the same question. The second stone mason replied, "I'm shaping this stone for a large building." When he walked a little further and came across a third worker with a smile on his face, the inquisitive child inquired with the same question. The third stonemason looked up with a polite smile and replied in a kind voice, "I'm building a marvelous cathedral!"

TAKE THIS JOB AND LOVE IT

The overwhelming majority of the centenarians we encountered experienced meaning, purpose, fulfillment and enjoyment in their work, whether at a business, factory, farm, or at home. Over 83 percent of them enjoyed their work "Very Much," and 16 percent of them "Somewhat" enjoyed what they did during their working years. Interestingly, only 1 percent indicated that they simply did not enjoy the work they endured their adult life and would like to have done something different.

If ever there was a delightful, enjoyable, and energetic "1 percenter" contrarian, it is Gordy Miller. At 100, Gordy is the world's oldest sailor. We visited Gordy and his lovely wife, Margaret, on a beautiful sunny day where you could see Alcatraz and San Francisco across the sparkling bay waters from their beautiful home.

Gordy was born in Santa Cruz, California, and when asked what is one of the greatest things about living to be 100, he replied, "Seeing all the changes in the world. The first plane I saw was a biplane. Man it was something!" He was in his early 20s when the Great Depression hit our country, but was spared a lot of the devastation experienced by many. "I was fortunate. I didn't suffer much. My dad always had a job, and when I got out of school I had a lot of silly little jobs. But I had jobs, and I worked, and it just sort of went by."

Gordy had strong work role models in his father and uncle. His father had a paper route as a youngster, and his uncle delivered papers in a horse and buggy. "Dad started a novelty shop that didn't work. Then he started a car service and I think drove the first car ever into Yellowstone Park."

Gordy Miller

He recounted having a lot of jobs early in his adult years. "I bought a Model T for $6—paid cash for it—and sold it for $12. I worked for Chevron for 13 years and retired with 75 shares of stock that really grew in value. My dad wanted me to go to college. I said, "No, I'm going to work and get an auto. I was young and wanted things."

When we asked Gordy about what he enjoyed most about his work during several decades of diverse labor, he immediately retorted, "To tell you the truth, I never liked working. I admire people who do. I worked because I had to. I had to earn money. I worked to enjoy my hobby and to take care of my wife and kids." And he has been sailing for over 74 years.

So, for Gordy, his work was a necessary means to a most enjoyable end—sailing. But he did it with excellence and purpose, which perhaps, in a funny sort of way, made his work not so unenjoyable after all. Gordy's definition of *rich*, with a big grin on his face, is "to have a wife that's really somethin' and children." Margaret was smiling, too.

With Gordy being an interesting exception to the majority of our centenarians, we were very pleased that most did enjoy their work years, serving as an encouraging role model for us. However, we did ask this question to expand our understanding about working over a century of living: "If you had your life to live over, would you pursue a different type of work?"

With the evolution of our society from a predominantly agricultural workforce in the early twentieth century, then to industrial and now to a predominantly technological/informational and service society, we thought that many of our centenarians would have chosen something different from the thousands of new-type jobs that have been created during their lifetime. But 80 percent said they would not have changed a thing. They chose well. They liked the type of work that was required for their vocation. Many of them would go into great detail with energy and exuberance and smiles on their faces as they described the specific type of work they performed, the bosses, co-workers and direct reports, and physical descriptions of the places they worked.

Approximately 20 percent indicated they would have pursued another career if circumstances had permitted them to do so. But, still, most of them were relatively pleased with their work experience.

The ABCs of Centenarian Jobs

Currently, the unemployment rate in our country is quite high. As previously mentioned, some studies suggest many Americans do not like their jobs/work. Often, in many situations, people become mildly to severely depressed when work is not challenging, rewarding, and/or enjoyable. It may cause them to lose resolve in wanting or even knowing where to look for work that could be satisfactory and enriching. The following composite of our many centenarian careers may give you or someone you know some information, hope, and inspiration to consider and research for half of your/their waking hours.

Centenarian occupations included:

A: aerospace director, advertising designer, attorney, accountant, auto mechanic

B: baker, banker, beautician, bookkeeper, butcher

C: cafeteria worker, caregiver, chemist, child care provider, clerk, cook, contractor, court clerk, construction worker/supervisor

D: dentist, dental assistant, designer, dietitian, drapery designer

E: editor, educator, electrician, engineer, examiner

F: factory worker, farmer, farm wife, fashion designer, food purveyor

G: government worker

H: hairdresser, hardware store owner/worker, homemaker, hospital orderly, hospital administrator

I: inspector, insurance agent, interoffice communication administrator, illustrator

J: jeweler, janitor

K: kindergarten teacher

L: laborer, landlord, legal secretary

M: manager, mechanical engineer, medical doctor, mill worker, minister, musician

N: nurse, nurse's aide, nursing administrator, Navy officer, nursery worker

O: office worker, office clerk, operator

P: paperboy, payroll clerk, piano teacher, policeman, printer, pulpwood dealer, purchasing agent

Q: quilter

R: railroad clerk, registered nurse, retail salesperson, road right-of-way agent, real estate agent/broker

S: sales, schoolteacher, seamstress, secretary, servant, shoe shop worker, stenographer, supervisor

T: tailor, teacher, telephone company worker, textile mill worker, tool-and-die machinist, truck driver, typist

U: U.S. Army officer, U.S. Department of Agriculture supervisor, U.S. Postal Service worker, U.S. congressman

V: Veterans Administration worker

W: waitress, warehouseman

As you can observe, our centenarians have contributed to many diverse components of our incredible economy over many decades. Many did what we would label as "physical work" during their lives. And the tens of thousands of inventions that they and their peers have created over the past 100 years has produced an exponential shift in the way we now do work. The encouraging dynamic throughout all of our conversations has been hearing how much their enjoyment of work positively impacted their view and enjoyment of life.

"Oh, I really enjoyed work. If you don't, you better get out of it,"
says Mable McCleery, 104.

FROM SUCCESS TO SIGNIFICANCE

"Every kind of work is valuable. It is just as important to dig a ditch as it is to sit in a corporate office. No work is disgraceful. Everything counts," says Clara Kramer, 104.

Change is a powerful word that brings thoughts of pursuing something different or even transformational. It can also imply moving steadily from one phase of life to the next, as all of our centenarians have done and are still doing. When you consider the changes in our workplace environment over the past 100-plus years, centenarians have earned high marks for tenacity, focus, and strong yet calm demeanor for succeeding through what they could not have imagined when they were young. As Isabel Thomas, 100, suggests: "When I was born 100 years ago, the world was a very different place. I have been a very lucky lady to have lived in a wonderful time of great change. I think my greatest attributes have been always to focus on the positive in every situation, to be adaptable, to work hard, and to be intellectually curious. I have had many interests, some of which are skiing, traveling, golf, and playing cards. Gardening and needlework were great passions also. I now have a Facebook page to keep up with the times. My motto to all is: enjoy life!"

When they began their working careers, there was no concept of retirement as we consider it today. In their early years of work, the eight-hour workday was just beginning

Clara Kramer

to catch on, but they did not imagine that they would ever be free to pursue hobbies or various fun interests in their "second half" of life as we anticipate today. Theirs was mostly an agrarian and industrial culture, where the majority of men remained in the labor force beyond 65 years of age—if they were still healthy enough to work. In 1935 the federal government decided to make 65 the age at which one could receive Social Security, even though the average life expectancy at that time was 63. Talk about a disconnect! This accelerated the whole concept of retirement in our nation.

During their early work lives, change looked substantially different than it does today. Most centenarians who began working in the early 1900s worked and received incomes without any concept or anticipation of the benefit plans that exist today in most public and private organizations.

As they have aged and matured through their working years, their definition of success at work has not focused significantly on financial gains or specific job-related accomplishments, albeit there have been many proud achievements in which they take great pride and pleasure. We did ask the question: "What was your greatest achievement at work?" Their variety of answers was delightful.

"Enjoyment of seeing the finished product."
ANTONIA DANNER, 101

"Having good crops."
EDWARD DAUBENSPECK, 101

"Feeling of accomplishment. Supported the Second World War
and Vietnam War by working and supplying the war effort
out of HAFB."
OLIVER MILLER DUNN, 100

"Having students remember me for years."
EVELYN FOSTER, 100

"Working with the president and country of Afghanistan."
LOUIS REITZ, 101

In addition to pride in work/job achievements and successes, along the way as they have pursued work with devotion and enjoyment, for many there has been a reordering of purpose and passion, resulting in a mental movement from success to significance whereby their work has become a more virtuous, fulfilling, and impacting contribution to themselves and the world around them.

Neither for them nor for us is getting "older" and surpassing 100 suggesting a mind-set of being "turned out to pasture." Rather, as our centenarians model, advise, and encourage us, we should become even more significant to ourselves and others with the incredible resources afforded us as we add mileage to our chronological odometer. Let's face it, at 100-plus you have a pretty credible platform from which to influence the younger generation. You have probably worked for good and not-so-good bosses, good and not-so-great organizations, hardworking and not-so-hardworking fellow workers, good and bad economic times, good and bad crops, surpluses, shortages, booms and busts—you name it. Centenarian status provides an expanded resume of time, talent, and treasure "capital" that is, in our opinion, priceless and needs to be shared with the younger generation for their learning and edification. This is a major reason we have dedicated ourselves to writing *Celebrate 100*, and encourage you to develop the same mind-set as you age wisely, excellently, and energetically toward the 100 mark.

Superignificant Superentenarian

Dr. Leila Denmark, a 114-year-old supercentenarian, beautifully models living life and approaching working with purpose, passion, success, and significance in a manner that is simply inspirational.

When we met Dr. Denmark and her gracious, energetic daughter, Mary—who is sure to be a supercentenarian also!—in their lovely home in Athens, Georgia, she exuded the charming and warm "bedside manner" that made her perhaps the most popular pediatrician ever in Georgia. She certainly was a successful physician from all traditional definitions, yet her greatest joy is still observing the enormous benefits

Leila Denmark

people derive from her significant and inspiring contributions and practical wisdom she has offered parents and children for almost a century.

She was born in a small Georgia town in 1898, the third of 12 children. She initially intended to be a teacher and attended Tift College to that end. But when her fiance, who worked for the U.S. Department of State, was sent to the Dutch Indies, where no wives were allowed, she decided to attend medical school. Her devotion and passion and commitment paid off by her being the third woman to be admitted to the Medical College of Georgia and the only woman in the 1928 graduating class. Upon graduation, she married and took a residency at Grady Memorial Hospital in Atlanta. She was the first physician on staff at Eggleston Hospital as it opened a pediatric hospital of Emory University. Later, she established a private practice and treated patients in her home clinic and continued her active medical career until the ripe old retirement age of 103! She has treated, inspired, and positively impacted thousands of children and parents, communicated in her book *Every Child Should Have a Chance,* a delightful and strongly opinionated treatise on raising children to be healthy both mentally and physically.

Another extraordinary, significant contribution she has made to our world is the vaccine for whooping cough. She glowed when describing her work with the research team that finally developed the vaccine for this serious medical infection that was killing thousands of people annually in the 1920s and 1930s. Conducting research in addition to her very full pediatric practice required many extra hours of work, but as she insightfully and energetically commented, "Work?! I'd never be idle. If you enjoy what you are doing, it is not work. I've enjoyed everything I have ever done." And this is one of her keys to happiness.

Dr. Denmark believes people are rich and successful if they have enough money to live on comfortably and help people. Money has never been a very important factor in her life. Her wise encouraging advice to all young people is "eat right and enjoy what you are doing."

Always a giver, she treated poor people at no charge. When we inquired about her fee schedule for treatment while practicing, she informed us, "I asked people to pay whatever they could afford. Some could pay the normal charge. Some couldn't. Made no difference to me."

In addition to her pediatric practice and research work, she still found time to do lots of charity work because, as she instructed us, "Where there is a need, find out how to settle it. If it needs money, give it money. If it needs time and work, give it both." Money has never been her motivation to succeed nor her means to significantly contribute to the human race. Helping children (and parents) live healthy lives is and always will be.

What a Work Ethic!

Our centenarians have strong opinions about working and enjoying work. Not only should we listen to their advice, we can learn from their examples. They have used brains and brawn to provide for themselves, their families, their communities, their country, and their world.

Martin Luther King, Jr., a luminary from this great generation, articulated their convictions well: "All labor that uplifts humanity has dignity and importance and should be undertaken with painstaking excellence."

Working' on the Railroad Man

At 114-plus, supercentenarian Walter Breuning was labeled by the *Guinness Book of World Records* as the world's oldest man. Born in Melrose, Minnesota, on September 21, 1896, Walter's family moved to Minneapolis, where he had his first haircut at age four. In 1901 his family moved to South Dakota. "My father was a civil engineer at a mill. There was no electricity at that time. I went to school, got to the 10th grade, and had to quit. My family broke up, and I went to work at age 14 at a bakery cleaning bread pans; $2.50 a week was the pay."

In 1912 he moved back to Melrose and went to work for the Great Northern Railway. He told us that he had to lie about his age—he was only 17 at the time—"because Jim Hill (the owner) didn't want nobody less than 18 years old." He had to hide and stay away from Hill for fear of being found out and fired but in 1918 was transferred to Great Falls, Montana, and has been there ever since. He worked for Great Northern until age 67, and was also a secretary/treasurer for the local Shrine Club. "I retired (from the railroad) at 67, but that was just one job. I've had two jobs all the time, so I've been busy

Walter Breuning

working. I was secretary of the Masonic Lodge." Walter signed up for military service in World War I but was never called in for duty. He wanted to serve in World War II but was too old to serve by that time. He was married in 1922 to his wife, Agnes, who passed away in 1957. When we inquired why he didn't remarry, he replied, "Oh, those second marriages never work—even most of the first ones don't work today!"

He has lived in the Rainbow Retirement and Assisted Living Center in Great Falls for over 30 years. Walter awakens bright and early and wears a suit and tie every day, looking sharp as a razor—as is his mind. He walks and talks with a sharp and accurate memory and strong opinion about everything. He eats only two meals daily—breakfast and lunch: "I only eat two meals a day. Been the same weight for 35 to 40 years. Get the weight off of you! Get down some more." He takes no medications except a baby aspirin daily, and finally had to obtain a hearing aid at age 111.

And he listens to talk radio programs most of the afternoon and early evenings, keeping up with the news, and is conversant on almost any subject you want to bring up. In 2009 he appeared on *NewsHour* with Jim Lehrer, offering his views about the newly elected President Obama and the state of the economy. Later, he was on the *CBS Evening News* in a special segment reported by Steve Hartman.

As we talked about the Great Depression and today's economic recessionary times, he had some strong perspectives. "I worked all during the Depression. You can't compare yesterday with today. No way. That's why the young people don't understand the 1930s when Washington tells them there's a depression today. Everybody's working (today) that wants to work. Listen (emphatically!), there's 10 million people right now probably out of work. Won't work. Can't work. Don't want to work. That's the way a lot of them are."

Sharing some of his advice about work, he enthusiastically articulated, "I tell people to stay in the work job as long as they can possibly work. I never retired until I was 99 years old. The last job I had was the secretary treasurer of the Shrine Club, and I quit when I was 99. I quit smoking at the same time." He jokingly commented that perhaps quitting smoking early has contributed to his longevity.

When asked if he enjoyed his work: "All the 50 years I worked for the railroad, I could hardly wait to get back to the job the next day. And as I said, two jobs all the time and I kept working all the time. I just loved to work. That's why I kept working till I was 99."

Since there is a lot of current research being conducted about work and its relationship to longevity, we asked Walter if he believed enjoying his work contributed to his longevity. "I think quite a bit. Working, I think, does the best for you that I know of. If you keep working, don't try to retire too early because I know people who retire and they want to fish and hunt and all that. Well, you know, you catch up with all that stuff in about two months and then there's nothing to do but sit, sit, sit. And that's what is no good at all. If you sit in the rocking chair too long, it won't be too long before you won't be there."

He energetically continued, "Work as long as you can and keep working because it doesn't hurt you. It's good for you—keeps your mind and your body busy always. Life just works better when you stay busy doing things. Helping others is the one big thing that I've done all my life. That's the best thing you can do—ever. If you can do something that's good for somebody else, you'll find it's good for you, too, in the end."

Adding even more inspiration and advice to our time with him, Walter challenged us with these words of encouragement: "When I retired at 99, I could have gone on for years because I felt so good. All my life I've kept up with things that are going on. I can remember back to when I was three years old. If you just keep that mind busy. You gotta keep that mind. The minute you stop using your mind and your body, you'll start deteriorating too—right away. Someday you'll find that out." That summed up Walter's "secret" to long life.

We hope you will accept Walter's wise, insightful, and inspiring advice: keep your mind and body useful and working, so you won't "find that out." As he so poignantly notes, "Life's length is not measured by its hours and days, but by what we have done while we are here. A useless life is short even if it lasts a century. There are greater and better things in us all, if we will find them out." Well said, Walter.

TEACHERS EXTRAORDINAIRE

Several of our energetic and interesting centenarians were educators, devoting their lives to teaching and influencing students to become productive citizens and contributors to our great nation. They entered their careers with a sense of mission and a desire to have a significant impact on many young people.

Work as Worship/Workship

When we attended the 100th birthday party of Thomas Glanton, there were so many former students, friends, and family present that we had to return later to conduct our video interview with this charming Southern gentleman and educator. He was born on November 4, 1911, in the first two-story house in Troup County, Georgia, a proud descendant of Oliver Cromwell, "Lord Protector of England," as he says with a grateful and proud smile on his face. Since his great great great grandfather had lived to be 110, "I wanted to live to be 100. On my 90th birthday, my grandson said, 'Pop, you'll make it,' and I did!"

Thomas Glanton

He was married to his lovely wife, Juliette, just two weeks short of 72 years when she passed away. He recalled the first time he saw her leaving a theater and turned to give him a look: "She gave me a big smile. That set my heart a-flutter." He has two children, four grandchildren, and nine great grandchildren, all of whom he is very proud. Thomas played golf till he was 87 years old. "I made three holes in one!" He drove an automobile until he was 97, his favorite country is Ireland, and his goal is to make it to 105 now that he has passed the century mark. We are betting he will make it.

His father was a gentleman farmer of 400 acres "when cotton was king." His 47-year-"young" father married 20-year-old Roselle Cleveland, who was a teacher in a one-room schoolhouse. All three of his sisters became teachers, so it was natural that he also pursued this noble profession. He took extra courses in high school and entered Auburn University at the young age of 15. "I took a five-year course in architecture and graduated in 1932. Architects were doing their own drafting and had let their draftsmen go. So I couldn't get a job. I lived a year with my mother and would pick up a little odd job every now and then painting signs for the city. One of the best jobs I had was on Fridays. One of the grocery men had a sale every Friday and Saturday, and I was paid a dollar to print copies of the sale signs and distribute them."

Even though it was during the Depression when he graduated from college and there were no steady jobs to be found in architecture, Thomas was determined to find work worth doing. "The back doors were closing, but the school building doors were wide open. So they needed a coach and math and geometry teacher. I taught geometry and physics and coached boys' and girls' basketball after school for two years. Then the principal left in late August to take a university job, and I was the only man in the school. So the Board of Education handed it to me and I became principal after two years of teaching." He later went on to earn a bachelor's degree in education and a master's degree in school administration.

Since he was a reserve officer in the military, Uncle Sam called him to Maxwell teaching aerodynamics to cadets in preflight school for 33 months. He was transferred to Intelligence School in Orlando where he was assigned to photo aerial intelligence operations. He was en route on the *Queen Mary* to Germany when they surrendered. Since he had the gift of writing, he was assigned a team of six stenographers to complete a study of the German air force. When Japan surrendered, he returned home and taught for 39 years during his distinguished educational career.

We asked his advice about managing money and finances. "Pay yourself first (save). Others second. The first year I taught, they only paid teachers $75 for nine months. That's $675 I had to live on from June till October. But, fortunately, one of the grocers had a young boy I had taught and he would carry me the whole summer. I didn't have any income the whole summer, and at the end of October when I got paid I would pay him $10 a month for what had amassed during the summer 4 months. And by the end of May, last paycheck, I had just paid him and had to start all over again."

When asked what he liked most about his work, with a wide smile he recounted, "The county school superintendent gave me these instructions the first day of my teaching. Now Tom, you go down there tomorrow and you teach books half the time and children the other half. And that's what I tried to do." Judging by all the past students that showed up for his 100th birthday party, he did a very fine job.

He absolutely loved his work, like Walter Breuning, and offered some of this sage advice to us youngsters: "Work hard. Play hard. And do the best you can with God's help. Put God first. Being around young people so long kept me young. And when it started making me old, I got out. You should, too!"

Of course, we asked him if he believed that enjoying his work so much has contributed to his long life. "Certainly. I wouldn't be here now if I had been an architect. I didn't build my cathedrals, but I took children out of a mill village and made ladies and gentlemen out of them." A pleasant glow of deep, enduring satisfaction swept over his face as he shared this nugget with us.

We asked Thomas to share his educator's advice with the younger generation concerning work and its importance to an enjoyable life. His answers were figuratively and literally inspiring. "Work is good worship. As a matter of fact, the word *worship* comes from the word *workship,* meaning relationship with God. So have a good "workingship" with God. Put God first, others second, and self last. Now that comes from the president of Auburn University. On Monday's convocation as a freshman I can remember him saying, 'Young men of Auburn, God has been good to you. You owe society a debt. Put God first, others second, and yourself last.' I've tried to do that." And he has done it well.

As we concluded our time with Thomas, we inquired whether he would have pursued another career if he had his life to live over again. With warm resolve he responded, "Teaching is the mother of all professions. I mentioned that my mother and sisters were all teachers. It runs in the family. The chalk dust on my shoulders is the 'badge' of my profession. As a teacher I was a member of the most challenging, most stimulating, and most satisfying professions in the world. The mother of all professions."

Health Pill

Don Robinson, 105, is the oldest living graduate of Boston College and can keep up with any freshman, sophomore, junior, or senior attending today! As full of energy and life as the day he was born, on January 14, 1908, in Massachusetts, he still lives in his home of 30-plus years, fixes a lot of his own meals, drove an auto until just a few months ago, reads, travels, goes shopping with his sons and

Don Robinson

lovely granddaughter Kim, watches television ("westerns are my favorite, particularly *Gunsmoke* and John Wayne"), loves visiting with people, and just simply enjoys life to the fullest every day with a smile and magnetic personality. Growing up in Brooklyn, New York, which obviously contributed to his tenacious and savvy mannerisms, he never gave a thought to living 100-plus years. "Probably the greatest thing (about living to be 100) is the fact that you made it and that you should be proud of something and that you were wise enough to take care of yourself to make it. After you've made it, then you can be grateful because everybody treats you differently. Now I'm treated, just jokingly, with more respect. They'll hold the door for you when you're 100!"

His secret to 105 years of abundant life is "moderation in everything—drink, running, sports. You get the toughest guy in football, that you envy almost in a nice way, he's gonna die at 78. No reason but he's worn his body out. Body is like a machine. My machine wears out. So moderation." He also points out that inheriting good genes can sure help the longevity process. Don is a role model of moderation in living, and he gleefully exclaims, "I haven't missed anything."

Don's father was a foreman in a shoe factory and insisted that Don attend college. "They didn't have a lot of money, but they put it in their son. Parents are wonderful, aren't they?" He attended Boston College and majored in social studies. Upon graduation, he decided to become a teacher ". . . right then and there. Evidently, I always knew that's what I would like to do. So I was hired and started teaching eighth grade."

He was always athletic: ". . . in my fashion and I enjoyed boxing. I was given the nickname 'The Fighter' by my students," which he touted with a bit of well-deserved pride. He absolutely loved his work as a teacher. "Your work is like a health pill. You go to work every day. You love your work. You're gonna live. If you hate your work, you're pulling your body and mind down. Love your work."

One of the things Don loved most about his work as a teacher was its steady nature, even throughout the Great Depression. "It was steady as you go for life. That's a pill right there. A doctor, a pill. Today, a man is nervous of losing his job. I was never going to lose my job all my life as long as I didn't break rules and regulations. So that was a great pill right there. Steady job."

"Another reason I loved my job was because I was communicating every day with very intelligent and nice people. I was learning from them to be nice. And also I loved it because it was a neat, nice, and lovely place to work. A school. It was clean, nice, and neat, and it was just wonderful to work in a situation like that."

When we asked him if he believed that enjoying his work so much had contributed to his longevity, he enthusiastically answered before we finished the question: "Oh, there's no doubt about it. Every day I was taking a health pill. I went to school and took a health pill. And being a teacher, everybody was nice to me. If you're happy, it's good for your system. Whether you're a teacher or your job (pointing to us) meeting people and traveling, you should outlive me!"

Don had an interestingly different answer to our request for advice to young people about work: "I read you should let children make their own choice, and then after that if you see they are failing, then you should come and try to rectify it. But you want them to pick what they in their own mind think: 'This is for me. I love it and want to try it.' Don't stop them and say, 'No, this is better, see?' Let them do what they want to do." Interesting advice to consider from "The Fighter."

Don was an educator for 42 years. "And that's why I have a good pension— 42 years." He loves and admires Franklin D. Roosevelt. "I hope he's in heaven. He was a wealthy, wealthy, wealthy man, but he kept thinking of the man in the street all the time (good advice for any would-be president). He had this law called Social Security, and they send me a check because of that wonderful man."

He never got into a lot of debt. "Fortunately, no. Not yet!" he says with a laugh. "But I've got another year to go!" Don says if he had it to over again, he would have been more of a saver. "I'd like to take a young person and say, 'Now save. Here's your bank. Did you put your money in the bank today? Save for the future so you can take care of yourself.'"

Transitioning from the Roaring Twenties to the Great Depression was like going from "normal" to "abnormal," according to Don. "Shifting into moderation kind of took care of me. I didn't fear it (the Depression) because I didn't want what I didn't have. So I was happy. I didn't have much but I used my judgment. I'm lucky, healthy, had good parents, wonderful friends, schooling . . . lucky. I didn't suffer because I didn't want anything—at least nothing I couldn't afford. I had enough of everything. Not a lot, but enough."

What are his keys to happiness? "At my age, that I can live in my own house, sleep in my own bed, eat my own food, cook, choose, have my guests in—so that's my happiness. It's my own little home and I love it." But he also has a very special "key" in his life: "God has given me something to help me. Absolutely. I can see it morning, noon, and night. He gave me a guardian angel. And I felt it twice." He went on to recount how his guardian angel protected him from serious injuries when falling on concrete a couple of different times. One lady who saw him fall thought he had died because the fall was so fierce. He jumped right up and greeted her with a smile and no injuries. "Some people laugh but I've got a good guardian angel." We're not laughing, Don. We should be so fortunate.

When asked how he would like to be remembered, Don paused, and then warmly responded "A loving friend to everybody I know, whether they are relatives or not. I want to be remembered as a loving friend." That desire is as guaranteed as 2 plus 2 equals 4. Certainly, you agree with us that Thomas and Don indeed succeeded in their quest for significance in the working chapter of their long and distinguished educational careers.

KEEPING UP AND KEEPING ON

As new inventions and opportunities continue to pour into our already busy centenarians' world, they continue to cycle on the Success to Significance continuum. Great motivators that help them stay active and promote new learning are technologies that provide stimulation to keep the brain sharp. They are models of how to stay connected to social networks, and they demonstrate to us that the work they have done and relationships they have created in their working years sets the stage for the marvelous ways we now connect and will connect in the future, regardless of our age.

Every year percentages increase as we ask about YouTube, TiVo, WiFi, text messaging, and other technological advances. If you think all centenarians are "not keeping up" with our perpetual progress, consider these encouraging data from our population of America's most senior citizens:

Lois Jones, 107

- Over 16 percent use cell phones on a regular basis. And no, they are not afraid of getting brain cancer from excessive usage!
- Over 25 percent use voice mail and love it (saves a lot of repeat calling).
- Almost 20 percent are using some sort of computer and actively sending and receiving e-mails (sure saves on postage). And remember, they were in their 80s and 90s when they started learning how to use a computer! So much for the "old dogs, new tricks" adage.
- Over 30 percent love to watch DVDs and listen to CDs. Their taste is as eclectic as a kaleidoscope.
- And almost all still like to watch television and/or read. No idle minds here.

So you can see that no moss is growing under the feet of these techno-savvy centenarians, and usage percentages among them are increasing annually as devices become more and more user friendly. The fastest-growing segment of our population is catching up with the younger generation technologically, which is opening wonderful doors of opportunity for sharing among generations "secrets," simple and profound wisdom, and advice and encouragement about work, money, and life.

WISE WORK ADVICE

Given their very diverse work experiences and number of years on the job, we asked our centenarians to offer some nuggets of wisdom and advice about work and jobs to younger people already in or getting ready to join the workforce. As with most of their answers on every subject, they are simple and straightforward. We are wise to take notes and listen attentively.

"Working is good for your soul as well as your wallet. It is good to stay busy."
ONEDA ANNE STREETER, 100

"Apply yourselves and do an honest job that is of good quality. Unless you take pride in your work, you cannot enjoy it. Money is not the most important element."
BILL MOHR, 100

"Be on time. Do not miss work unless you have to. Do an honest day's work for your employer."
LOUISE CALDER, 100

"Choose the type of work you are capable of, and that is consistent with your physical abilities, talents, and mental abilities. Choose the kind of work you think you would enjoy—indoor versus outdoor, with people or with machines."
FLOYD ELLSON, 100

"Do the best you can and work hard. Give your employer their money's worth."
VIRGINIA SCHULLER, 100

"Do your job to the best of your ability and keep your mind on what you are doing. Always give a little more than is expected of you."
GLADYS HOLMSTRAND, 100

"Enjoy what you do. Work hard. Appreciate the opportunities that are available. Take advantage of opportunities, especially for advancement."
HELEN DESPOTOPOULOS, 102

"If not pleased, change. Do something you enjoy."
JOE STONIS, 100

"Start each day with optimism and enthusiasm. Give it your best and always be honest."
ISLA JENNINGS, 100

So what are the secrets and wisdom we glean from their advice on work? Competence (IQ [intelligence quotient]) skills and knowledge are important. They must be thoughtfully considered in selecting work that fits your level of ability for the job and, of course, interest.

However, character (EQ [emotional quotient], the ability to manage ourselves and relationships through self-regulation, motivation, empathy, and social skills) is equally if perhaps not even more essential. Approaching work with a sense of pride, doing more than is expected, enjoying what you do (or change), being enthusiastic and optimistic about the possibilities of achievement, and always being honest will result in a working career well lived no matter how long you are on the job.

Working Through (a Century of) Bumps in the Road

Not one of our centenarians experienced "smooth sailing" in every season of their expansive lives. There have been bumps in the road for all of them that have impacted their work and personal lives. As they transitioned from buggies to automobiles to airplanes, paper-and-pencil desktops to keyboard laptops, some were fortunate to have quick and easy access to these constantly changing resources, while others experienced various barriers that prevented easy access to new inventions and expanded work opportunities.

Many of our centenarians expressed that they wish they could have obtained more education for career/work opportunities. Almost 75 percent completed elementary school, 65 percent completed high school, 10 percent attended some sort of trade school, and approximately 35 percent completed a college degree program. Their strong advice to the younger generation is to obtain as much education as possible to enlarge and enrich your career options.

But educational regrets, wars, the Great Depression, health issues, and many other challenges have *not* stopped them on their career journeys with a positive and grateful and determined attitude. Their perception is that with all the technological advances and educational opportunities existing today, the younger generation has no excuses for not seeking, finding, and enjoying meaningful and significant work in our expanding domestic and global economy.

"Take advantage of opportunities that come your way. Don't be afraid of a reasonable and practical amount of risk after due investigation. Acceptable opportunities may not present themselves again," says Nelson Nieuwenhuis, 100.

We asked our centenarians how they coped with life's ups and downs in the middle of work, wars, and constant rapid change. What advice would they give to younger people about overcoming life's difficulties. What wisdom could they offer about accepting work struggles, challenges, and opportunities. Just like us, work consumed half (and in many cases more) of their waking hours, and they had to juggle the interruptions and idiosyncrasies of life while staying committed to performing their jobs with integrity and satisfaction.

Over and over again, their responses emphasized similar and simple themes that the younger generation can derive such great benefit from if incorporated into their mental worldview and their daily actions:

- Be willing to work hard—all the time.

- Do your personal best no matter how seemingly significant or insignificant the task.

- Cooperate by helping others.

- Accept help when needed—pride is foolish and hurts everyone.

- Don't procrastinate.

- Get your work done before you play—you enjoy both more that way.

- Do what you like and it's not work.

- If you don't like what you do, find something else.

A majority articulated that to enjoy work for many years, or most of your life as in the cases of a number of our centenarians, does take a lot of faith, optimism, and a "take life one day at a time" attitude.

"Life is what you make it. No one can do it for you. Have pride and love yourself. Do your best work like it was your own business," says Sophie Birk, 103.

Tough Times Don't Last but Tough People Do

Our centenarians are very aware that political decisions have affected their working opportunities and circumstances both positively and negatively over the past century. Of the 21 presidents they have seen elected, Franklin D. Roosevelt, who served from 1933 to 1945, was the favorite among the majority of our centenarians, both Republicans and Democrats. They cited that his optimism and activism brought new spirit to a burdened nation. The New Deal was designed to produce economic relief, recovery, and reform by providing lots of government jobs and also stimulating growth in the private sector workforce. Many of our centenarians expressed the exact same statement in response to our inquiring why Roosevelt was their favorite president: "He gave us hope!"

Making a living through the Great Depression was difficult for many people as unemployment rose to 25 percent at the peak. But we heard many stories of how positive determination and kindness people showed to each other enabled them to overcome life's difficulties—including financial burdens—in this turbulent time of our nation's history.

Centenarian Gold Mine

In our travels throughout the country, we were incredibly fortunate to discover a virtual "gold mine" of wisdom, wit, stories, and advice at Mount Vernon Towers in Atlanta. This lovely senior living facility is home to five—yes, five—charming centenarians who graciously welcomed us on our centenarian quest. Maxine Brown, 104; Willie Foster, 101; Garnett Cobb, 101; Rosalie Wolosenka, 101; and Mable McCleery, 104, could fill a library with their 500-plus combined years of work, fun, adventure, and life lived much more than "half full."

Rosalie Wolaskena

Mount Vernon Towers Ladies

Maxine Brown was born and grew up in Pensacola, Florida. She attended Florida State University, was married 49 years ("I had the best married life"), drove until she was 94, and had a red Chevy for 18 years, which she loved. She did have an aunt in New Orleans who lived to be 104, but when we asked her if she ever thought she would live to be 100, she retorted, "Never thought I'd live. I was a preemie and weighed one and a half pounds. They should have thrown me out." We are glad they didn't, as she is chock-full of energy, wit, and wisdom. "I don't feel my age and I don't act it, unfortunately! Some days I feel my age, but most of the time I feel fine."

When she graduated from college, she was a bookkeeper for a while. Then she got married and moved to Buffalo. "I didn't like the cold and snow, but Al had a job."

When asked about her advice to young people about work, Maxine energetically said, "I think they should all work and know the value of living. When we got married they were only hiring people who were married, and the husband had to be working. And I had very good recommendations. They said, 'This is wonderful but we can't hire a woman.'" She went on to share about their managing life through the Great Depression. "Al was an engineer and he worked for Titus. We helped other people, we hired people—we had a man on the block. He would clean the snow. I wish he could have taken it with him (she giggled). But anyway, he came to collect on Saturday and we had him in the house and gave him a hot lunch and sent food home with him. All the people on our street were young people, and at Christmas we would get a family and help them. They didn't know who was doing it. We were so young. We knew we were OK, but we did help everyone we could, and a lot of times some of us would get together, make a lot of soup, put it in quart jars, and just put it on our steps. It was terrible because I have never seen it before. I never want to see it again."

Willie Foster, 101, was born in Alpharetta, Georgia, now a booming populated suburb of Atlanta. But, as she points out, "It was the country then. I was raised on the farm. My daddy died before I was born. My mother had seven children, and all of them went to the field to work. But when I was born my older sister stayed at the house and Momma went to the fields to show them what to do."

Her favorite job on the farm? "Hoeing. I didn't really like to, but I *had* to! (laughter) I worked in the fields and tried to take off Saturdays and Sundays." But she went on to say that she worked many weekends to make ends meet.

In discussing the Great Depression, Willie talked lucidly about the challenges of working on a farm. Even though many people living on farms did not experience some of the extreme difficulties of city dwellers during the Depression, she pointed out that "we had to make it. Just went out and worked hard. I had an older sister, and when we got able to work, we had to hire out and pick cotton. One day picking cotton over near the highway, I picked about 300 pounds of cotton. And I told everybody I know that I picked more cotton than she did (my older sister). At least I thought I did."

"We had cows, horses, plenty of bread and milk, nothing fancy. We raised our own beef, we had hogs and meat, so we never went hungry."

When we asked her advice to young people about working she was pretty pointed as she recalled her working times as a young adult. "Make 'em behave. Children today don't have to work like I did. That makes a lot of difference. Just work! Don't sit around and be lazy. Work at whatever. We had to make it. I picked 300 pounds in one day." (She mentioned that 300 pounds of cotton a couple of times!)

Mabel McCleery, 104, loved to play golf. "You couldn't play too much golf. After I retired, I loved to play golf." She was born in Georgia in 1907, one of seven children. "No one in my family that I know of ever lived to be 100." Mabel had a 100th birthday party that was "so great it took me weeks to get over it. I could not believe it, and I mean there were people from everywhere. But I haven't found anything that's as exciting with the 104." She drove until she was 93, and her favorite car was a powder blue Thunderbird: "Whoooooeeeee, it really bugged me to give up my love car. And it still does."

She worked for about 16 years with a wholesale manufacturing company that made ladies' hats. "That was interesting. We had to work hard to hold our jobs—we really did." Mabel worked at a number of different jobs throughout her working years, but the most interesting and enjoyable job she had was that of a dental hygienist. "I was a dental hygienist. I did other things up until then, but a friend of mine was a dental hygienist, and I was determined to be one, too. So I started studying under this doctor and then I went to work for him. I happened along at the right time. It was during the war and jobs were hard to get."

She stayed in that job for over 15 years. Did she enjoy her work? "Oh, I really enjoyed that work—and if you don't, you better get out of it. I liked meeting different people. You meet some of the finest people. I don't know if I succeeded in making them feel good but I tried." Given her bubbly personality, our bet is that a lot of folks actually enjoyed their visit to the dentist when Mabel was there to greet them and say, "Open wide."

In giving advice to younger people, she echoed many of our other centenarian friends. "Try to get what you enjoy the most. And do the best job you possibly can for whatever you decide on. That's the only way I know to do it. I really enjoyed my dental work. Don't know if it contributed to my longevity, but it was a good way to make a living."

Her memory of the Great Depression was not particularly negative, due in part, we believe, to her positive and tenacious attitude about life. "I always managed to have something to do. We didn't have a gourmet menu, but we got by with what we had. That was just the bare necessities mostly. I had some bad times and good times—I had some pretty bad times, but I just hit it head on!"

She was insistent on us sharing her advice with the younger generation about managing money. "I saved up and paid cash. I didn't want to owe any money. I wanted to pay as I go. I paid cash for about everything. I didn't buy it if I didn't have the money. Now that's something to tell the young people. Don't buy it if they don't have the money. So many of them go in debt and, oh, just eat themselves up with debt. And that's not good, I don't think. I did without. They should, too." Wise advice, we believe, for working and living with less worry.

Garnett Cobb, 103, was born in Danville, Illinois, in 1909. The oldest of four children, she lived in Indiana and Florida before moving to Georgia, and has written a book on the history of Sandy Springs, Georgia. Although her mother died at the very young age of 34, her father lived to be 84, and she had a great aunt who made it all the way to 105. The greatest thing for her about turning 100 was that "you get so much attention!," she exclaimed with a giggle and laughter. "I got lots of letters and cards, and over 250 people came the first hour of my birthday party." Although insisting she has no secret to living 100-plus productive years, she points out: "I'm very interested in life."

She was married for 60 years and has one son living in Georgia. "We never fussed. We weren't the fussing kind." Her advice to young girls about marriage is sage: "I always heard if a man is good to his mother, he'll be good to his wife, or if he's good to his wife, he was good to his mother." She is a strong advocate for marrying because you are in love, not because it is convenient.

She drove a car until she was 96 in the busy metropolitan Atlanta area, and quit voluntarily. "The kids didn't make me give it up. I was on my own." She turned in the keys herself. Her favorite car was a dark red Mercury sports car, "but I never got a ticket."

She worked in the banking industry for 32 enjoyable years. While she was still in school, a friend called offering her a job. She told him that she had not finished school yet and was probably not yet qualified, but he insisted that they would teach her everything she would need to know. "So I left school because a job was more important in those days than it is now."

Her advice to young people about working harmonizes with most of our centenarians: "I would tell them to like what they do—to love what they do—and then give it everything they've got." She emphasized with a smile, "I loved what I did. Every minute."

Being a banker, we asked Garnett to share her financial advice with the younger generation. "I'm sorry to say a lot of people are in debt over their heads and they don't realize that until it is too late. You don't buy anything unless you can pay for it." Even though she was in the banking business, she and her husband never borrowed a lot of money. They used credit cards but paid them off at the end of every month. "We didn't believe in paying interest." Paying cash definitely reduced stress in her life, which she believes contributed to her long and enjoyable life. "Watch what you spend. I've got a lot of Scotch-Irish in me. And enjoy what you spend." Great advice from a very seasoned banker.

Fortunately for Garnett, as for a number of our Centenarians, she was not negatively impacted severely by the Great Depression. "I knew people were jumping out of windows and carrying on, but I just wasn't into it. I really didn't realize what all was going on. Everybody was in the same position. You didn't feel like you were rich and you didn't feel like you were poor because everybody was suffering the same experience. My dad had a big garden, cows, chickens, and about six pigs. So we had plenty to eat." She did recall that gasoline and some other items were rationed, but for the most part she just worked hard right through the Depression—a common centenarian theme that is very relevant to all of us today in these recessionary and challenging financial times.

Rosalie Wolasenka, the proud daughter of Polish immigrants, was born in the Big Apple in 1910 and grew up with a brother and two sisters. Her father died at 39, her mother at 64, and she never knew anyone in her family who lived beyond 60-ish. She was married 65 wonderful years, and her husband lived to be 90. Her greatest thing about living to be 100? "That I'm living! That I'm in good health. Oh, there are little glitches here and there, but I think everyone has those. But nothing to complain about (another common centenarian comment)." In stark contrast to Dr. Leila Denmark's secret to living 100-plus years ("Ever since I was 7 months old I've drunk nothing but water"), Rosalie is just as adamant: "Never drink water. I seldom drink water. I make myself a cup of tea a couple of times a day." She occasionally has a glass of wine, and when her husband was living would periodically enjoy a sip of Scotch, but "we are not drinking people."

She moved to Georgia at the age of 90, and on her 100th birthday "my niece gave me the most gorgeous party anyone ever had here. They're still talking about it. She had over 100 people here and made roses for everyone out of ribbon. She had a seated dinner for over 100 right here on the sun porch. So after that, I said, "This is my hurrah—a Joe Kennedy quote—that's the end."

She graduated from high school and worked in a few different places, taking the trolleys and buses to and from work. "I always felt safe. Sometimes I came home at 10 or 11 at night, but no one ever bothered me."

She worked at Macy's for a couple of years as a cashier in the Tube Room, but it was boring work, so she moved to Gimbel's department store. "I was a saleslady there. I was selling ladies' gloves and sundries. Whatever I did, I enjoyed. I always enjoyed my work. I made it my business to be friendly with people. I always was and that's about it. What can I say? I tried to be happy and I tried to do well, and I still do things that way. I still enjoy doing whatever I can. I've always had hobbies of some sort." Indeed she has. Rosalie was an athlete, running low hurdles and high jumping. She loves to dance, reads books, makes vases and fills them with flowers for gifts to people, and can "still thread a needle," making beautiful glass bead flowers and decorations, always staying busy.

Her perception about and advice to young people today about work is worth considering whether you agree with her or not. "I think the average person starting a job today is annoyed he has to work. He doesn't like the idea of working for anybody. And that attitude is very bad when you start to work. You're angry before you even begin anything." Her remedy for this approach to work is: "Have a different way of thinking. And don't believe all bosses are tyrants."

Rosalie also weathered the Great Depression quite well. "It didn't affect me at all outside of seeing people selling apples at street corners. I was married. My husband worked steady. I didn't see anyone starve to death." Perhaps her and her husband's staying debt free, and waiting to save enough money to pay for their house in cash, helped weather of lot of the storms. She says, "We never even had a mortgage."

She also has a strong faith in God. "I tell Him, 'Any time, take me away.' I say, 'What are you doing—redecorating my apartment again?!' I think He listens to me. I tell Him to wake me up at 8 o'clock in the morning and at 8 o'clock sharp I wake up without an alarm." A very special centenarian indeed.

More Nuggets of Work Wisdom

Harry Adler, 101, shared with us that his mother died when he was two weeks old, and his dad left when he was a baby. An aunt and uncle adopted him and made him start working at age 10. The highest grade he attended in school was eighth grade, and he remembers coming home from school, changing his clothes, working on trucks, and returning home at 11 o'clock at night. He was held back in school three times because he could not complete his homework all the time and was told he was dumb. "No one helped me stop being treated like this." How did he work through his bumps, ups and downs? "Just accepted it," he said warmly without any accusatory or resentful tone in his voice. Centenarians just don't blame others for their vicissitudes of life.

Noah Dupont, 101, told us that he attended school until the sixth grade, then needed to help his parents with income for the family, so he went to work. His sage advice about work is: "Enjoy what you do, but know that you can't always be happy."

Harry Adler

Elsie Rich, 106, philosophically and poetically shares: "I always liked to work, so I was happy. In the winter of my life, my thinking is 'Spring, eager to learn what the next day will Bring. And when it comes to the end of the Road, I wish you are told she lived many years, but she never grew Old.'" If we adopt Elsie's attitude about life and work, life cannot be much richer or more enjoyable no matter what is thrown at us or just comes our way.

So take heart from our seasoned class of centenarians. As you hit those inevitable bumps in your road of work and life, keep on cruising over them with hard work, determination, best efforts always, accepting temporary setbacks, developing a strong faith and optimistic spirit of hope, living fully one day at a time. All work is "workship" and is indeed a best prize. Do it with gusto and adventure, and you greatly improve your possibilities for a century-plus of enjoyable and significant life.

CHAPTER 5

The Top Secrets from Our Centenarians

SECRET 1: ATTITUDE

SECRET 2: HEALTHY EATING

SECRET 3: FAITH

SECRET 4: EXERCISE AND ACTIVITY

SECRET 5: CLEAN LIVING

SECRET 6: FAMILY

SECRET 7: GENETICS

ADVICE TO CENTENARIAN WANNABES

WHY 100?

In 1513 Ponce de Leon began searching for the legendary Fountain of Youth, and ever since then people have been intrigued—in many cases obsessed—with discovering the mystical "secret formula," "magical pill," or "eternal elixir" for extending life into a perpetual panoply of blissful youthful existence. Whenever we mention our research and interest in centenarians to anyone anywhere, the immediate first question that everyone wishfully asks is: "What's *the* secret?" We always smile and calmly suggest, "Read our book."

As you have read through the pages of *Celebrate 100* to this point, we hope you have gleaned that there is—in our opinion, at least—no single secret to making it 100-plus years. As we extensively articulated in Chapter 2, many factors contribute to the centenarian "formula," and hundreds of millions of dollars have been and continue to be invested into serious scientific and medical research in an effort to determine the key marker(s), factor(s), secret(s)—whatever you wish to label them—that will enable people to extend life to 100 and even well beyond that initial notable benchmark of aging. The majority of centenarian research we have observed throughout the scientific, medical, and general media has focused on the roles of diet, exercise, social relationships, and inherited DNA as it pertains to your likelihood of extending life and achieving the 100 milestone. Not only are we the biggest cheerleaders and encouragers of this funded research, but we want to be first in line to take "the pill" or whatever regimen that provides high probability of centenarian and supercentenarian achievement.

Our research efforts have been less rigorous quantitatively, scientifically, and medically, but more focused on narrative, historical recounting, and qualitative thought and perspective directly from the 500-plus centenarians we have personally interviewed, videotaped, and surveyed. We have not taken blood or DNA saliva samples, measured heart rates and blood pressure pre-post rigorous exercise routines, or administered psychosocial instruments measuring longitudinal stress levels or interactive family/social dynamics. These are all necessary and important quantitative scientific research methodologies that can enlighten our society about aging possibilities and lead willing participants to longer lives of healthy living.

However, we have extracted hundreds of hours and a few thousand pages of fascinating stories from the heart, memories from the mind, and nuggets of century-old wisdom and advice that are instructive, commonsensical, helpful, encouraging, motivational, and inspirational to everyone who will incorporate them into their daily dosage of living.

This chapter will offer the "distilled essence" of our qualitative centenarians' responses to the question we asked of them about their perceived "secrets" for living such long and productive and enjoyable lives. In a sense, we are trying to present to you a smorgasbord, or perhaps a rainbow of secrets that both scientific/medical research and our narrative/historical recounting research has yielded. Until we learn more and discover the definitive quantitative formula for vastly extended longevity, you may select and prepare your own diet or pick your own colors and paint your personal picture for living many more years than you contemplated before reading *Celebrate 100*.

If you choose and implement with enthusiastic anticipation, the journey will be a long and lovely joy ride, delicious and colorful, worthy indeed of wonderful celebration.

On the Internet you will find hundreds of articles and highlights of research reports offering a plethora of clues, tips, steps, ideas, suggestions, and so on for how to reach the magical age of 100. This literature addresses your family genetic history, gender, exercise regimen, social interaction, levels of worry, age of childbearing, weight, diet, attitude, and a host of other sound bites, all of which may be helpful to your centenarian journey. Our approach was to simply ask each centenarian we interviewed and/or surveyed the simple question: "What is your secret to living to be 100?" (Or whatever their current age was at the time of questioning.)

Many gave immediate answers with incredible levels of confidence and resolve. For instance, supercentenarian Dr. Denmark, 114, immediately informed us her secret was drinking only water since she was seven months old. Lois Jones, 107, replied that eating chocolate and sipping a little wine daily was her secret. Some would initially suggest they didn't have any secret(s) or have any idea how they had lived so long. But on gentle prodding and insistence, we captured a perceived answer from almost 100 percent of them. By design we had established no predetermined set of categories. Our goal was to ask them the simple question, register their response, and create the categories as they evolved.

As we tabulated all the responses, seven "categories" of perceived secrets, from the centenarians themselves, emerged in rank order of importance. Granted, this is not rigorous, quantitative scientific research, but we believe it is very important, informative, and encouraging as you seek to assemble your own "menu" or paint your personal "picture" of a centenarianship quest. These category labels are ours, not necessarily theirs, but we hope they communicate to you the distilled essence of their self-perceptions and answers.

SECRET 1: ATTITUDE

Almost 100 percent of our centenarians believe a positive attitude about life is important, if not essential, to success and longevity in life. Over time, their attitudes have changed and expanded as a function of emotional responses, behavioral tendencies, and deeply held personal beliefs. Most of them have acute perceptions, are very discerning—we like to call it *savvy*—and possess a uniquely wise understanding about life that perhaps only a century-plus of living can provide. As Loren Greiner, 100, shared with us, "I am pleased to be a centenarian. My thinking power perspicacity (intelligence manifested by being astute) seems to be holding up."

We marveled at the positive mental attitudes of most centenarians we met. About half of our centenarian class described themselves as *optimistic*, and the other half labeled themselves as *realistic*, in a positive sort of way. Over 60 percent claimed the label *happy* when we asked them to pick a word or two to describe how they have felt and still feel about life after so many years. Many others endorsed the words *content*, *hardworking*, *thankful*, *level-headed*, *adventuresome*, and *caring* to frame their outlook. Whether optimistic or realistic, these special people have become productive human beings who have progressed far up the attitudinal developmental ladder. Indeed they are mature citizens who embrace all that life offers with an attitude of gratitude.

We recognize some people argue that positive mental attitude is tough to measure or quantify, but we can assure you that "you know it when you see and experience it." One centenarian pointed out that there are essentially two kinds of people: Those that wakeup in the morning and enthusiastically say "Good morning, God!!" and those that begrudgingly wake up thinking, "Good God, morning," with a sour demeanor. Most of our centenarians are "Good morning, God" people even though they have lived through the Great Depression, multiple wars and recessions, financial and health challenges, and personal heartaches, just like many of us. The majority embrace each day of life as a gift and a blessing to be savored and enjoyed to the fullest.

For the most part they have mastered the art of not worrying, even though they have had plenty to worry about over a century. They just chose not to sweat the big or small stuff. Many of them pointed out to us that attitude is a choice. It's up to you. Nobody else can choose or do it for you, no matter what your personal circumstances. They have chosen to embrace a positive, refreshing, thankful attitude toward life. The large majority of our centenarian class said this was their number one secret to their long and productive and enjoyable lives.

"I think stress will kill you."
ETHEL BARNHARDT, 101

"If you have peace of mind, that's all."
ELSIE RICH, 106

"Worry isn't helping the situation any, and if you can't do anything,
forget about it because worry only brings lines to your face."
ELSA HOFFMAN, 102

Harold Rowe

We hope you will emulate our centenarians and learn the discipline of not worrying. It just may be your most important discovery to centenarian achievement. And as our wise elders have insisted, "It's up to you."

Harold Rowe has one of the most positive "can do" attitudes we encountered in our travels throughout the country. Born near Troy, New York, in 1910, he started Rowe's Cleaners, which he ran for 35 years. Then he began a second career with the county sheriff's office using his photographic skills for criminal investigation and documentation. He is a life member of the Troy Elks Lodge 141, where he has served in many different capacities. Harold also founded the St. Jude's Horse Show to raise funds for his church and school, and worked with the Boy Scouts of America for over 50 years. If anyone deserved to be featured on the Smucker's jar with Willard Scott on the *Today* show, it has to be Harold—and he was in 2010 on his actual birthday, March 3.

He told us that his secret for making it to 100 is "working hard and taking care of your health." With a great deal of humility and well-deserved pride, he shared with us how he started his first of several careers that extended late into his 90s.

"I was driving a truck for another dry cleaner and I was getting $20 a week. I said, 'Geez, I ought to be able to do something better than this,' so I got to know all the customers. I had $25 in my pocket. I borrowed $100 and I started in business and I ended up over $100,000 in debt." Most people would have thrown in the towel and probably declared bankruptcy at this point, but Harold's determined optimism and achievement attitude pushed him forward.

"But I worked out of it. I worked at that business 35 years. It started in a little hole in the wall and ended up in a two-story brick building that used to be a hotel. I had 16 people working for me and I had two trucks."

When the Depression hit, his "can do" attitude and persistent hard work continued to reward him. "I prospered under the Depression by building my business up. I don't know how, I was just terribly lucky. People were suffering and I was getting better. I worked like the devil."

Like most of our centenarians, Harold really enjoyed his work in spite of the long hours and tough times through the Depression because "I was accomplishing something." After leaving the dry cleaning business, he took his love of photography and went to work with the sheriff's department, where he worked until he was 72. "I was supposed to retire at 70, but due to my ability the sheriff wrote a letter to the state requesting an additional year and they granted it. Come another year, they wrote another letter and they granted it again. On the third year, the state said 'no,' that I was supposed to retire at 70 and they thought I had done my job."

You catch a little more of a glimpse of Harold's tenacity, optimism, and attitude toward life and work with his final "chapter" of employment. "I would have liked to continue working (for the sheriff's department), but when I left there I went to work for an undertaker. I drove the hearse and I worked there for 20 more years. That's when I retired."

When we asked him why he wanted to continue working so long with such energy and devotion, he humbly replied, "I wanted to get ahead. I wanted to be proud of myself. I enjoyed my work—it was a learning process. If you don't enjoy getting up and going to the office, don't do it."

Moving to Georgia to live with his daughter and son-in-law after 96 years, no wonder his hometown of Wyantskill, New York, misses this leader and landmark of their community. But, according to Harold, being married to his lovely wife Julia for 76 years was one of his greatest accomplishments.

SECRET 2: HEALTHY EATING

Hundreds of books, thousands of articles, millions of commercials, and billions of dollars flood our society promoting the benefits derived from eating healthy foods. The overused familiar adage "You are what you eat" has never been more omnipresent from dining rooms to schoolrooms to boardrooms. The Food Network is one of the most popular cable channels, viewed by tens of millions of people daily. And as our dear friend Truett Cathy, founder of Chick-fil-A insists, "Food is essential to life, therefore make it good."

Dining, Not Dieting

Now please note that *diet* was *not* the second-highest perceived secret for longevity by our centenarians. It was healthy *eating* in moderation. We asked every centenarian if they had ever been on some sort of controlled diet program—Weight Watchers, Nutrisystem, Jenny Craig, and so on. An overwhelming 78 percent responded that they have never been on any kind of what we would call a diet program or plan.

Most of them have always eaten, and still do eat, whatever they want in reasonable, moderate portions. As Daniel Merlini says, "Eat whatever you want to eat, just eat less. That's all you gotta do."

Their menus cover most of the food chain: water, wine, coffee, chocolate, red meat, fish, chicken, barbecue, fruits, vegetables, hot dogs, hamburgers, candy, desserts, ice cream—the entire culinary kaleidoscope. A few of our centenarians are vegetarians, but the majority are carnivores—although in moderation. And many of them still cook. Les Oldt, 107, bakes bread regularly and serves up some lip smackin' ribs almost monthly. Don Robinson, 105, still loves to go shopping and prepare a lot of his meals at home.

And remember the sound advice of Helen Toomey, 104: "Chew your food. Don't just take a bite and swallow it."

"Eat the right foods and exercise," says Anna Orr, 100.

Lessie Smithgall said with a laugh, "Saving water and drinking wine. I have had a good diet all my life. I have taken good care of myself."

Jim Kelly, 101, was as pointed as one can get: "You have to try and have good health. And you cannot have good health if you try to drink a lot or booze or you try to take drugs. You just make sure you get a good piece of bread and a cup of coffee."

Scout's Honor

In 2007 Marianne Crowder was hailed as our nation's oldest living Girl Scout. She was born in Colorado Springs, where she grew up and acquired a love for dance, which motivated her to open and operate her own dance studio and head the dance department for Colorado College before marrying and moving to California in 1939. Marianne taught in Stanford University's drama department for 19 years and choreographed dances for many major productions of the drama and music departments. She continued teaching dance until she was 97 years young and still lives independently in her lovely home in Palo Alto, California.

Marianne Crowder

When we met her at the door, it was shocking to see someone look so fit and at least 25 years younger than what we knew her actual age to be. Her secrets to 100-plus years with such youthful appearance and vitality were several. "I think dance has really helped. I have a good disposition and I've had a good life. Whatever I've gone into has been successful. I have no complaints."

We inquired if she has ever followed any special diet regimen to generate such vitality. "No. I don't like fatty foods and I don't like a lot of meat. I'm sort of squeamish unless it is something nice. I eat mostly fruits and vegetables. I'm not keen about fish. I like steak (she says with a wink and smile). Well, what other kind of meat is there?!"

Living at home, she still prepares most of her own meals. "I was a good cook, but I didn't favor being a cook. I really do like simple food—but it can be too simple (she says with a laugh). I always eat breakfast. I have always liked outdoors and do a very little bit of gardening. I used to sew and knit very well. And I read volumes; I like biography."

Asking about her greatest successes in life, she responded with pride and appreciation: "Well, I've always been on top. If it's dance, I've been the best. If it's Scouts, I've had the highest honor. It hasn't been that I thought I was better, it's just that it's been more fun for me and I had a gift for it."

Scouts and dance were great avenues for her to stay active and in shape, but dance brought her the most joy in life. As she entered the decade of her 80s, she published a book and video entitled *Mariantics,* which describes and demonstrates dozens of exercises and nutritional suggestions to keep you in shape for life. And she is living proof of her work. "I feel 40-something in my mind," she says with a smile. We asked for copies of her book and video!

SECRET 3: FAITH

Faith in God or a higher power was prevalent among the majority of our centenarians. Mostly coming from many Judeo-Christian backgrounds, they expressed extreme gratitude to God or their higher power and attributed their faith as the secret to their extended years of enjoying family, friends, careers, travels, and activities. Dozens

Ruth Crumley

articulated how their strong faith has sustained them through both good and excruciating circumstances: from surviving a Nazi concentration camp in World War II to overcoming tragic family losses and life-threatening illnesses during their century of living. And while enjoying life today with a positive attitude, most look forward to their "next chapter" of life, which is a foundational cornerstone of their faith.

Ruth Crumley, 101, simply smiled and exclaimed, "I don't have a secret. The Lord just hasn't called me yet."

Emma Victoria Johnson brought a laugh when she insisted, "The Lord doesn't want me (yet), and the devil doesn't want me either!"

Eloise Wright, 100, shared her secret with a warm smile, "Being a servant to others and letting the Lord take care of me."

Harry Steine, 100, was brief: "Do your best and trust in the Lord."

And Louis Reitz, 101, summed it up: "God is there. Contact Him."

Reverend Luke Kot

Ora et Labora—Pray and Work—Till Death Do Me Part

Reverend Luke Kot, the oldest of a fellowship of Trappist monks at the Monastery of the Holy Spirit in Conyers, Georgia, is still going strong at 101. Our visit with him was truly inspiring and instructional as he shared with us his life before and after coming to Georgia and helping build the monastery beginning in 1944. He enthusiastically and energetically lives his life by a centuries-old motto: Ora et Labora, which means "Pray and Work." And he starts early. "We used to get up at 2:00 A.M., and sometimes 1:30 and even 1:00 A.M. Now we get up around 4:00." Kot lives with the 40 monks who share his faith and enthusiasm for prayer and work, praying seven times daily together.

Brother Luke, as some choose to call him, was born in Montana, the son of Polish immigrants. "The young boys would shout out at me, 'A cowboy, a cowboy.'" He had three sisters, all of whom lived very long lives. His father lived to be 94, and his mother 86.

When we inquired how he decided to become a monk, his story was intriguing. "I knew that I wanted to be a monk from the time that I was seven years old. There were factories around us (his family had moved to Niagara Falls, New York, by that time). I wanted to get an education first, so I went to high school but I knew I didn't want to go to college. My purpose was I wanted to work in a factory for at least five years before I joined a monastery." We asked why he wanted to delay his entering the ministry, and his answer was surprising and refreshing.

"I worked five years purposefully so people couldn't say I was a lazy type of person and just wanted to go to the monastery. I did the most common work. I swept floors. The manager came to me one day and said, 'I've never seen anyone with so much work and passion with a broom. You're the first person to keep the floor clean. You've done an excellent job." With a grin, he continued, "I took the lowest job. They wanted to promote me. I didn't want it. I wanted to stay in that common job. Then I went into the monastery and have been here till this day—over 73 years."

Along with the other monks who came to Conyers from Kentucky, he helped build the monastery literally from the ground up. "I laid stones and built a wall. Work to me— laying stones and cinder block—was joy and happiness. I liked it. I didn't mind it. Work was never a curse to me. It was always the best thing in the world because God created us for good works."

We asked him what is the greatest thing about living to be 100 and he shared: "Just living life and enjoying it while you have the grace of God to live. You should be happy about life and not disappointed because you are aging. That has never bothered me. When I wanted to join the monastery (most were in Europe at the time), I happened to mention to the Lord that 'if you find a monastery in the United States, please let me know and I will enter "till death do *me* part.'" And He took those words and that's the reason I'm living so long. He's holding me up because He's making me live those words out!"

He went on to share his secret to long abundant life that pertains to all of us. "In the first chapter of the St. John's gospel, he has a little sentence in there. It says—God is love. Period. And if God is love, He loves us so much and He wants that love back to Him. So He puts us for a short period of time on this Earth and we have to prove that we love Him, too. And we have a place to test this in this life. If you are doing that, loving others, then blessed are you because you are living and doing what He expects of you . . . so you can have life eternal hereafter."

All we could think to say in response was "Amen!"

SECRET 4: EXERCISE AND ACTIVITY

Like we do with food and diets, Americans spend billions of dollars annually on exercise equipment and programs to look good, stay in excellent physical shape, feel better physically and mentally, and, ideally, live longer. This is a very positive trend to overcome the obesity and unhealthy eating habits affecting our population. Exercise and activity ranked fourth in our centenarians' frequency of perceived secrets for their exceptional longevity. But their definition or approach to this category of secrets is not quite the same format most of our younger generation approach exercise and activity.

Less than 30 percent of our centenarians have ever been on any kind of prescribed or special exercise program or regimen. The ones who have experienced those professionally designed and administered programs have very much enjoyed them and feel they have greatly benefited from their commitment to and involvement in them. But for the vast majority of our research group, their "exercise" was simply part of their ordinary daily work activities, whether on the farm or in the cities. Very few were joggers or cyclists, but most were walkers—in many cases, looooooooong walkers—crop pickers, sweepers, window washers, stair climbers, gardeners, chore performers, or whatever their home or business circumstances demanded. Most of them have stayed mentally and physically active in their "gymnasiums" of everyday life. As we cited in an earlier chapter, many worked well into their 80s or 90s, and some into their centenarian years. Many still cook, walk, read, attend cultural events, and engage in active social settings to stimulate their mental and physical faculties.

Garnett Beckman, 101, astutely suggested, "Keep moving or you cannot keep moving."

"Enjoy life, be active in sports to keep up your physical condition, no smoking, moderate drinking,"
suggests Noah Dupont, 101.

Active "Mermaid"

Helen Hannah's four lovely daughters describe her as "fiercely independent," which is part of her makeup that has kept her so alive and active for over 100 years. At her fabulous centenarian birthday party, over 150 friends and family from all over the country came to celebrate this gifted lady, and she exclaimed, "I was 25 years younger on that day than I am now!"

When we visited Helen in the lovely Atlanta home she has lived in since 1951, we asked her what advice she would give the president of the United States, having now lived a century through 16 different presidents." She immediately replied "Stay active!," which is the hallmark of her life. "Stay active as much as you can. I went as long as I can remember to water aerobics three times a week. I couldn't go for a long time after I fell, but I just now started back about two weeks ago." She invited us to attend one of her sessions, which we did a few days later. It was a full, non-sissy aerobic workout with a group of her "young friends" in their 80s and 90s.

"I stay active here in my house. I did all my own yard work for years and years. Even when my husband was living, I did most of the yard work. I cut the grass on the lower level and on the front. (It is a big yard!) And I planted the flower borders all across the back and up the steps. I had it looking real pretty."

Helen went to work right out of high school and pursued photography as a career. She was the premier portrait photographer in Lynchburg in the 1930s, running her own business out of her mother's home. She described going into business for herself as the best financial decision of her life. "I had

Helen Hannah

my workroom in my mother's basement, and I used her dining room to set up my equipment and take pictures there. I enjoyed my work. Loved every minute of it. People would come to me from all over to have their photograph."

Another piece of Helen's active life is her love of travel. "I used to go everywhere, all over the world. Any time someone would say 'Come on, let's go,' I'd go. My first trip to Europe, I was 27 years old. I just sort of got into the habit—I liked it—and started going every year."

For Helen, the greatest thing about living to be 100-plus is "the devotion of my children. Don't know what I would do without them. All four of them. They are the sweetest four girls that have ever lived in this world, and they'll do anything for me." Although the first in her family to reach 100, we doubt that she will be the last, given the vibrant, active legacy she has established for her family.

SECRET 5: CLEAN LIVING

When we asked Loren Cartwright what was his secret to an energetic 100-year lifespan, he looked straight in the camera and meticulously articulated with energy and gusto, "Good clean livin'!"

There is no question that this label can be defined an infinite number of ways, but as we listened to our centenarians and tabulated their responses, "clean living" was the phrase that we chose to identify this fifth-most-frequent number of responses to the secret question. So we won't belabor an attempt to define the theme in detail, but we believe most of you will get the picture.

Almost 75 percent of our centenarians never smoked, and of the ones who did at one time, most stopped between the ages of 40 and 70. Walter Breuning was obviously the contrarian, smoking till 99 and living to 114-plus. No one is an excessive drinker or drug user, and no one has any serious criminal records.

Charlie Surrey, 101, was getting ready to go fishing with his younger brother (95) when we visited him. His answer was simple and pleasant. "Eat right, sleep right, and don't get mad."

Charlie Surrey

"Just stay out of trouble. That's all," says Harry Adler, 101. Good advice for everybody at every age.

We loved Essie Smiley's 100 wrap on this secret: "Clean living, no alcohol, no tobacco, plenty of sex." There's probably another whole book possibility with these thoughts!

Aunt Pauline Copeland, 100, echoed this theme with "hard work, clean living, no drinking or smoking or late hours, and faith in my heavenly Father."

Edythe Thompson provided a thoughtful response for this category: "I suppose good heritage. Clean living, no smoking, a little drinking, and eating plenty of chocolate."

Numerous other comments echo these similar words and phrases, constituting what we label *clean living* as one of our centenarians' top 7 secrets to their special chronological status.

"Keep the 10 commandments, moderation in everything, treat others as you would have them treat you; clean life, happiness, exercise, good food, good friends, good church home; clean living, friends, and God; lead a quiet, productive life. No bad habits. Go to bed about 9:00 or 10:00. Get up at 7:00."

"Live right, live for God, and treat your neighbors right."

We believe it is worth your while to glean these comments and create your own *clean living* definition for contributing to your personal centenarian "menu" or "painting."

3 DOs—3As

Kathryn Dwinnell has always contemplated living to 120. A devout Christian lady who is very knowledgeable of the Bible, she pointed out that in the book of Genesis, Chapter

Kathryn Dwinnell

6, verse 3, it states that our ". . . days will be a hundred and twenty years." Thus her consideration of 120, and as she explained, it doesn't matter if you make it or not. "It is something that could happen. I know beyond the shadow of a doubt that God can do anything. What I don't know is will He with me." Whether she reaches that supercentenarian number or not, her 107 years so far have been as full and representative of clean living as anyone we know. "I do know that I have to do my part. You have to take advantage of what God offers. So I'm doing my part. I'm exercising. There's many times I'd much rather lay down on that daybed than go downstairs and exercise. But I need to go exercise. I'm eating right . . . pretty much—I still like fried foods (she says with a smile). A friend asked me if I would like some 'fried food.' I said, 'Sure.' She brought me 'dried prunes.' Background noise really interferes with my hearing!"

Born August 26, 1905, in Nebraska, she grew up with five older brothers on a farm. "I arrived ahead of the doctor. He was delivering another baby somewhere else in the county and I couldn't wait!" She still lives in Lincoln, Nebraska, was married 70 wonderful years, and has four children.

Kathryn possesses an optimistic, enthusiastic philosophy about life no matter what the circumstances. When asked about her surviving the Great Depression, she offered some wise advice from experience, not theory. "Back in those days we lived on the 3 Dos: Make Do, Do Over, and Do Without. But we really didn't do without. We did without luxuries and things that weren't necessary. You rip something up and make something else out of it. Also, you have to Adjust, Adopt, and Accept. Now that's something the Lord has given me. I can do all three graciously. Don't think of the things that you've lost. I just think with a grin of the places my red shoes have been," she chimes with a winsome smile from ear to ear.

Her secret to such a long and joyful life so far? "I do think my attitude. I was born with a good attitude and I think attitude makes a world of difference. You can take what somebody says as an insult or putting you down, or you can take it as just a statement and more or less a compliment. We had a friend whose language would curl your ears, and he would often say to me, 'Katie, you're a strong old biddy.' And it was a compliment. Being called an old biddy could have insulted me, but instead of that, I loved to hear Jennings say that. So you see, it's how you take things, and I think attitude makes all the difference in the world."

The greatest thing to her about passing the century mark is that "Everyone is so nice. They all want to take care of me. Did you notice how those servers catered to me today at lunch? Years ago, I said that I was lucky. Now I say I'm blessed. There is no such thing as luck."

She has a very simple definition of *rich:* "Being loved. Having friends. There is absolutely no one who has been nasty with me. I have everything I need, and I have no worries."

Like most of our centenarians, Kathryn has paid for everything she can think of in cash—except for a washing machine, vacuum cleaner, and their first house. "We had a 10-year mortgage on our first home and paid it off in 9 years. We had two children and decided to buy the vacuum cleaner and washing machine 'on time.' Washing on that board was quite a chore." We believe that is about as legitimate a reason imagineable for buying something 'on time.'

If Kathryn had the opportunity, she would share her 107-plus years' seasoned advice to the president as follows: "Ask God before you make any move, and do what He tells you." You don't need to be president to heed and implement that sage suggestion.

SECRET 6: FAMILY

As we mentioned in Chapter 2, a great deal of longevity research highlights the perceived importance of community, social support systems, and family to the overall mental and physical well-being of individuals. A lot of our centenarians defined the word *rich* (Chapter 3) as a loving family and close family relationships. When the word *family* emerges in conversations today, emotional responses range from high blood pressure to contagious smiles of pure pride and joy. Certainly, a good, happy, healthy family life situation contributes to a more enjoyable *quality* of life. But might it also positively impact the *quality and quantity* of our years?

Our centenarians seem to think so, ranking it sixth as a key secret to their long life, and an encouraging reason for wanting to live even longer, enjoy the love of family, and leave a legacy for them to possess and cherish. Hearing centenarians speak about their families warmed our hearts. Most have vivid and detailed remembrances about the good and challenging aspects of their family life when young and as the father or mother of the family they created.

It did not surprise us to hear them articulate that commitment, communication, appreciation, spiritual growth, "healthy" stress, and family crisis management are essential ingredients to strong families. The intimacy they still give and take to family is a key part of their continuing social development and enjoyment. We heard over and over again in affectionate terms how their spouse or children contributed or still contribute to their physical, mental, and spiritual health today.

Interestingly, over 65 percent of our centenarians grew up with three or more siblings, yet over 60 percent of them have two or fewer children. They have followed our national trend of smaller families, but overwhelmingly say family is vital and is the nucleus of their life. Following are some typical responses to the question "What activities do you most enjoy today?"

"Reading and family visits."
Marguerite Ranard, 101

"Church activities and family."
Emma Markert, 102

"I walk, shop, cook, and do as much as I can with my daughter and son-in-law. Seeing the grand and great grandchildren."
Albina Sacchetti, 104

"Honoring my parents and family."
Carroll Dietle, 100

So, as you can see, for many of our centenarians, healthy, loving families make the difference when the ups and downs of life occur, and are invaluable to their ability to survive and thrive into their "platinum" years.

Bertha Wolfe, 104

Nelson Nieuwenhuis, 100

Fern Groh, 102

Emma Markert, 105

Besse Cooper, 116

Wise and Witty Centenarians

SECRET 7: GENETICS

As we reviewed earlier in the book, much research and study continue to inundate our scientific and medical world in efforts to determine the genetic linkage and predictability for living longer, and how to replicate the longevity genetic structures in people who are not so positively genetically inclined toward beyond-average life expectancy. Much scientific research suggests a strong correlation between people who have parents or siblings with long lives and their likelihood of the same, but many of our centenarians came from families with no family members living beyond their 60s.

Still, a few of our centenarians perceived that good genetics was their secret to living to be 100 and beyond.

"I came from a family of longevity."
LEO BALEY, 100

"Born with good genes and led a pretty healthy life."
ALICE FROEMMING, 101

Andy Weinandy, 100, laughingly replied, "I picked the right parents and genes!" Of course, his comment flew straight in the face of our friend Gordie Miller, who astutely observed, "It's hard to pick your parents."

So if you come from parents or grandparents with good long-life genes, or have siblings who have lived or are still living very long lives, consider yourself very lucky. You possess a higher probability than many of living long and reaching 100 or more.

But even if you are not so fortunate to come from a "genetic powerhouse" family, do not be discouraged. Neither did a large percentage of our centenarians, and the best news is that you have the other top six secrets that you can creatively, enthusiastically, and diligently incorporate into your daily schedule that will vastly improve your likelihood of getting into the centenarian club. In addition to these seven top categories that most of our responses created from the secrets question, there are a few jewels that we thought you needed to know about just in case none of the others appeal to you:

- "A wonderful and loving family, the good Lord, and a rum and Coke every afternoon."
- "I do not know. I wish I did. I would sell it!"
- "I am just lucky."
- "Mind my own business."
- "My biggest job is to keep myself healthy. I question even drinking too much coffee. And I like coffee!"
- "Not dying."
- "Regular table tennis, moderate eating, and I really believe that my marriage at 95 to a lovely woman 28 years younger than myself has made all the difference in my life."
- "Relaxation and a sense of purpose."
- "Take as little medication as you can."
- "Vinegar and honey."
- "Keep breathing!"
- "If I told you, it wouldn't be a secret!"

We thought these would add to your smorgasbord and rainbow of secrets satisfaction and enjoyment.

ADVICE TO CENTENARIAN WANNABES

Many different questions were asked in our encounters with these marvelous people, all seeking to capture wisdom, wit, insight, and advice about money, work, and the many various aspects of life from their unique, long-term perspective. Since repetition is the "mother of all learning," some answers may seem repetitious to you. They are. We want to ensure that you do not miss their simple but profound answers because they reflect not only living 100-plus years chronologically, but living 100-plus years wisely and well.

One of the questions we asked, somewhat related to our secrets question, was: "What advice about anything would you give to people who think they might want to live to be 100?"

Yin and Yang: Being and Doing

Most of their responses distinguished between what we must "be" and what we must "do" to enhance our possibilities for making it into the centenarian ranks with enjoyment and a sense of fulfillment. They are two aspects of an integrated, whole human being about which much has been researched and written in popular psychological and business literature.

As we reflected and listened to them articulate their advice for centenarian "wannabes," it became apparent that their wisdom is about both *being* in the flow of life, patiently allowing it to happen, while at the same time *doing* life in an intentional, straightforward "make it happen" way with steady determination and resolve.

We believe this yin-and-yang full approach to living well and living wisely is no secret, but rather a reasonable series of practical choices made over a 100-year lifetime. Almost half of their advice to wannabes emphasized the importance of having a sound sense of *being*. About a third of their suggestions highlighted *doing*, and the balance of responses incorporated both fairly equally.

"Be faithful and trusting. Take it one day at a time."
LOUISE HARRY, 102

"Be accepting of what life brings and try to make others
glad they passed your way."
Rebecca Williamson, 100

"Be your own health advocate. Do not smoke and drink—seldom
if at all. Live near people who are interested in your welfare.
Participate in activities, sports, games,
driving, clubs, etc."
Floyd Ellson, 100

Bill Mohr

Bill Mohr's father died when he was 3 years old. His sister was 18 months old. "It was absolutely awful. We didn't have anything to eat at all. We knew what it was like to have just one meal a day. But we never took it too seriously." He joined the Army in World War II at age 31 and received the French Legion of Honor Medal. "From a physical standpoint I was in good shape. I had all my teeth. Not a cavity in one of them." He was injured in Europe, had surgery on his back, and "I had to learn to walk all over again. But the doc said I recovered better than anyone." After the war he worked in several careers, retiring at age 93. "I loved my work, and they loved what I did. You have to enjoy your work if you want to get both pleasure and compensation from your work. I loved it."

He shared some very wise advice to centenarian wannabes. "Find pleasure and joy in all your neighbors. Don't be envious of your neighbors if they have a new car and you don't. It's all relative. See something beautiful in your surroundings. I was never envious of anybody, and there was no poorer kids on the street than my brother and I—none. Take one day at a time. Life is very big. What seems like the end of the world in your twenties, you won't remember when you are 80 or 90. So relax and enjoy your youth.

"While living to be 100 is quite a bit in the genes, try to take life one day at a time. It is probably not the amount of years you live but the quality of life you put into whatever years you are blessed with." Well said, soldier. Good orders for us all to follow.

*"Eat properly. Only drink on social occasions. Keep active mentally.
I read the* New Yorker *and the* New York Times *daily, play bridge
with friends, and walk at least five times a week several blocks.
Get checked by doctors and dentists regularly."*
ANNE HALLEY, 100

*"Hang in there, think positive, eat what is good for you, exercise,
be happy, count your blessings—they are many."*
FERN GROH, 102

*"Enjoy your life, friends, and work. Stay as healthy as you can. Do not
drink or smoke. Keep it simple and as stress free as possible."*
MAYNARD ANTHONY WHITE, 101

"Keep active, do things now *while you can do it so you can keep on doing it.
Keep satisfied and enjoy each year one at a time."*
FREDERICK GREEN, 100

*"Three things: Maintain a healthy lifestyle, enjoy your
family and friends, do nice things for others."*
LOUISE CALDER, 100

We hope these few quotes that are representative of hundreds more suggestions are encouraging and heighten your centenarian wannabe desire. Not only will your journey to 100 be full of enjoyment, you may be delightfully surprised after blowing out all those candles.

WHY 100?

Occasionally, we meet people who, when discovering our interest and research on centenarians, ask this question in a somewhat sarcastic tone: "Why in the world would I want to live to be 100?" Perhaps never having met or read about active centenarians, they cannot imagine that anyone over 100 years old can still be doing much that is really fun. As you well know by now, they could not be more mistaken. Many of them are still having fun, energetically enjoying life and looking forward to each new day of life they are granted. Some of the fun activities they still enjoy and enthusiastically enjoyed telling us about included:

"Discussions with people who think."
MARVIN KNEUDSON, 100

"Ride my bike, play organ, music director for church."
LOUIS REITZ, 101

*"Cooking, crocheting and knitting; also writing letters
to my relatives and friends."*
FRANCES JACOBS, 100

*"Reading my Bible and other Christian literature,
crossword and circle word puzzles."*
ANNA ORR 100

*"Reading, having friends visit, exercise class,
jigsaw puzzles."*
DORIS PARKER, 102

"Visiting with my family, flowers, and bird watching."
ANNA MARIA FIERRO, 100+

"Golf."
HELEN MACDONALD, 103

"Making crafts, watching television, and playing cards."
CATHERINE ANNA HABRAKEN, 101

"Attending Quest—a community for lifelong learning."
RUTH PROSKAUER SMITH 101

"Playing games, being with friends, doing my volunteer work."
MARION RISING, 101

"Visiting with friends, talking about old times, listening to music, and watching people dance."
BESSIE MINTON, 106

"Dancing, watching international news, fraternizing with neighbors."
RICHARD MORRIS, 102

"Sew new clothes."
STELLA KARTT, 102

"Bingo, reading, visiting with friends and family."
IRMA FERGUSON, 100+

"Lodge work and church volunteer at food bank."
MARY KUHN, 100

"Baking bread and flying with my son."
LES OLDT, *107*

"Making glass bead flowers and rag blankets."
ROSALIE WOLOSENKA, *101*

Pauline Copeland, 100

So you can see there is no moss growing under these centenarians' feet. They are living testimonies to just how long and vibrant and interesting and meaningful life can be if you approach it with a positive, optimistic mind-set. We hope you agree that they are encouraging answers to "Why 100?" and that by now you are a raving centenarian wannabe. You have the secrets, wise advice, and glimpse of what life up to and beyond 100 can enjoyably look like. Now you just need to "catch the spirit."

Esther Robinson, 101, and Mary Stalnaker, 101

Emma Johnson, 102

CHAPTER 6

The Centenarian Spirit

You've Gotta Have Heart

THE CENTENARIAN SPIRIT

THE CENTENARIAN SPIRIT IN ACTION

RENEGOTIATING LIFE

SPARKS OF THE SPIRIT

CENTENARIANS ON THE GO

KEEPING LIFE INTERESTING—COMMON INTERESTS, NOT COMMON AGE

CONTEMPORARY CENTENARIANS—THINKING AND FEELING YOUNG

CATCH THE SPIRIT: FORGET AGING GRACEFULLY—AGE EXCELLENTLY!

A FORMULA FOR LONGEVITY

A TOAST TO FUTURE CENTENARIANS

"You've gotta have heart
All you really need is heart
When the odds are sayin' you'll never win
That's when the grin should start"

"HEART" MUSIC & LYRICS BY RICHARD ADLER AND JERRY ROSS,
FOR *DAMN YANKEES*, BROADWAY MUSICAL, 1955,
DIRECTED BY GEORGE ABBOTT (WHO LIVED TO BE 107 YEARS OLD)

What do Elsa Hoffmann, Verla Morris, Rosie Ross, and Will Clark have in common? What they have in common is heart. It's an intangible, but you feel it when you sit with them and hear their stories—theirs and a zillion stories of their peers, all of whose words resonate with the spirit that comes through in the lines from the song in *Damn Yankees.*

When Rosie Ross, at 101, takes the stage at the supper club in Prescott, Arizona, and raises that shiny new trumpet to his lips and belts out "Sugar Blues," or puts on the mute for "You Made Me Love You," and then sits down and talks with you about how much he loves performing, with a bourbon and a splash of water in hand, you know you've met the real thing.

When Elsa Hoffmann, at the age of 100, goes out and buys herself a purple Lincoln for her birthday, invites 150 friends and family to her party, and then takes off on a Caribbean cruise, there is no mistaking that this is a lady who reflects the words of the song.

When Will Clark and his wife, Lois, glimpse the Pacific as they transition from Highway 10 from Arizona onto the Pacific Coast Highway headed to San Louis Obispo to visit their son, there's no question that these two centenarians are really enjoying life.

When Verla Morris logs on to check her e-mail every morning and then chats with new friends on Facebook, we can see that this is a lady who is not intimidated by new technology at the age of 100.

These centenarians and their active contemporaries shatter the long-held stereotypes of aging as a dismal time of life and give us a new, optimistic view.

Heart is a quality that is omnipresent in centenarians. We call it "The Centenarian Spirit." It is an inner belief, a philosophy of living that comes from practice, from experience, and—yes—from wisdom. Although it is metaphysical in concept, it is immediately recognizable in our centenarians. You can hear it in their words, see it in their daily actions, read it in their stories, and feel it in their presence.

Heart is at the essence of being an active centenarian. It is what allows them to happily and enthusiastically embrace life, even in circumstances that others would find difficult or inadequate. It's what makes life worth living. It's their ability and potential to be extraordinary. To go from ordinary lives, for the most part, to extraordinary elders and role models for enjoying life and living it to the fullest. They do not feel sorry for themselves or for their circumstances. They find pleasure and acceptance in the lives they have lived. Centenarians choose to be happy about their lives and about themselves. Most say they are satisfied with their lives and have found a sense of fulfillment in their later years. It's what allows them to find joy in just being alive, and gratitude for the extra time, the extra days, to spend with family and friends, to accomplish the things that they still want to do, and to add to their legacy.

The components of *Heart* are found in The Centenarian Spirit.

THE CENTENARIAN SPIRIT

The Centenarian Spirit offers a platform from which we can learn to live a long and healthy and happy life. It is a combination of five essential characteristics. These are common among the centenarians in this book wherever they live, their gender, whatever their past or present station in life.

1. **Love of life, which includes a sense of humor and a healthy dose of self-esteem.** Centenarians have a zest for living life in the moment and to its fullest. Their creed is: Enjoy each day!
2. **Positive yet realistic attitude.** Our centenarians believe you get farther in life and enjoy it more by being positive and realistic.
3. **Strong religious or spiritual belief.** Centenarians are grateful for their long lives and cherish every day they have. Most have faith in a higher power and look there for guidance.

4. **Personal courage.** Living long takes courage. Life deals everyone difficult hands over the years; whether a serious medical condition, or economic misfortune, for example, problems simply have to be faced and the challenge taken on—so easy to say, not so easy to do.

5. **Remarkable ability to renegotiate life at every turn.** This requires resilience, adaptability, and willingness to accept the losses and changes that come with aging, including losing loved ones, and not letting it stop them. Centenarians are not quitters. They do not give up on life during hard times—they cope.

THE CENTENARIAN SPIRIT IN ACTION

The Centenarian Spirit in action illustrates the will to see life through to the best of one's ability. It is the joyousness of Madeleine Turpan, the optimism of Aline Matthews, the lifelong religious faith of Williett Bracey, and the moral compass of William Thomas. It's the determination of Rosie Ross, and the resilience of Mary Tysdal. While different in nature, each of these individuals possesses the mettle to persevere throughout their lives.

Love of Life—Madeleine Turpan, Star of the Bristal

"Joie de vivre" is the first impression everyone gets meeting Madeleine, a vivacious 100 year old. "Yes, a lot of people tell me that," she says. "I don't do anything special; it's just the way I am." Pausing, she says with a mischievous grin, "Perhaps it's my French heritage. My mother came from Paris."

Madeleine grew up in New York City near Central Park. "I married at 19 in 1932. When I first got married I wanted to go back to school, but my husband wouldn't let me—he said I had enough education. He was Armenian, with a large family living in New York. They spoke their language when together, and I was left out. Worse, I didn't know what they might be saying about me, and as a young bride this made me uncomfortable. So I bought a first-grade book and taught myself Armenian well enough so I could at least follow their conversations without them knowing.

"For 35 years during our marriage I worked for Stouffer's restaurants in New York, primarily as the chief dietitian at Top of the Sixes, a prestigious restaurant at that time at 666 Fifth Avenue. I was the overseer for all of the food preparation. Mrs. Stouffer was ahead of her time. Most of the cooks and employees were women.

"We never had children. When my husband retired, we traveled a great deal and we both enjoyed that, especially trips to Europe. But once I was widowed, I went back to school in my mid-70s. I wanted to fill myself up with more than movies. I went to LaGuardia and had to start all over again with high school. I graduated with honors and then went to Hunter College in New York for two years, commuting into the city from Long Island."

Madeleine now lives on Long Island in at a large retirement center. "She's the center of attention," her nephew Gene says. "Everyone loves her." "You can't help but feel better when she's around," adds an admirer, a gentleman who is almost 99.

Recently, she was interviewed by the radio station at a university near her home for her views on life at 100. On air, both of the students remarked on Madeleine's "joie de vivre"—those exact words. "It was a long interview, but I liked it," Madeleine relates. "I was the oldest person either of them had ever met—or even thought of, I suppose."

On the day of the broadcast, Gene (who is her frequent companion) and she listened to it in his car, parked in the lot of one of their frequent hangouts, which they call "The Castle." "It was interesting hearing my voice coming out of the car radio—a first! It went on for at least a half-hour. I hated to hear me end," she says, and expressed her desire to do it again.

"Then we went in (the White Castle) and celebrated with a cheeseburger, fries, and coke. We go there frequently. Everyone is friendly, and of course they all know us. For my 100th, they threw a surprise party for me, and really went all out with big balloons

Madeline Turpan

and the whole place decorated. It was very nice of them and we all had a lot of fun. Then later, of course, my family took me to an elegant restaurant where we had my official celebration. I enjoy both—the casual and the formal lifestyle. I always have. I never thought I'd live to 100, I have to admit, but I love every minute of it!"

Positive Attitude—Aline "Stretch" Matthews

Aline "Stretch" Matthews was born and raised on Long Island. "I'm not sure how I got this nickname," she says, "but I've had it all my life. Maybe it's because my father was the chauffer for a prominent family and drove their limousine—my friends might have picked up on that."

Stretch tells of her idyllic childhood living on the waterfront estate. "It gave me a taste for elegant clothes and an elegant lifestyle. Fortunately, my husband was able to provide that, and we traveled for his work, taking our son and daughter with us. We traveled worldwide and finally settled in Venice, Florida. I still am very particular about my clothes, my apartment, and my presentation overall. And I'm still getting a weekly massage, as I have for the past 50 years, ever since I heard of its health benefits. I would describe myself as very outgoing and gregarious, and I like martinis at fine restaurants and going on other outings. I can handle the unexpected challenges that come my way from time to time."

Plans for a party to celebrate her 100th birthday escalated. A favorite niece and her daughter were coming from San Francisco and several other relatives were converging from different parts of the country. Stretch looked forward to dinner with them at a nearby restaurant that she had chosen. One of the guests was concerned that at her age perhaps it was better for her to stay home and have the party there and not venture out. Indignant, Stretch immediately replied: "I'm going! Don't count me out yet!"

Later, she told her niece, "I don't know who said this, I'm sure it's not original, but I think pessimists die early."

Religious/Spiritual Belief—"Big Momma" and "Granpy"

Williett Bracey is known as Big Momma or Mother Bracey, depending on which of the two pillars of her life one is referring to, her family or her church. She was honored at the Methodist church in Jackson, Mississippi, that has been her second home since she was nine. "I went to the elementary school here before going to high school. I've been a Sunday school teacher, treasurer, secretary, and also president of the Women's Society of Christian Service (now called United Methodist Women). I've put on a lot of fundraisers over the years, the most recent two years ago where we raised $5,000."

At home, Big Momma raised six children. "I still shepherd—well, ride herd on—my extended family, and I still cook Sunday dinner after church," she says. "They all come. They love my cooking."

Of the many amazing things Williette has witnessed in her life, she says she never thought she'd see a black president. To her, that's been the biggest advance in her lifetime.

Her advice on living a long life is simply to "trust in the Lord and do what His word says, and I believe that's why I'm living this long. I can't tell what's in my future, but I can tell you who holds it. I'm just going to run on and see what the end looks like."

Of her 100th birthday, she says it was her favorite ever. And for now she's happy the Lord has left her right where she is. "I'm planning on buying a big flat-screen TV with my birthday money."

Heart of Gold—"Granpy"

William Frederick Thomas, 101, now known as Granpy by everyone, was born in Bridgeport, Connecticut, and created a nice life for himself, on his own. He became an optometrist and an amateur watch repairman. "I liked precision, a place for everything and everything in its place kind of guy. I guess that's what made me a good pilot and flight instructor, too, which I took up in my 40s and really enjoyed. I married, had two daughters; life was pretty normal.

"Then my wife passed away and I remarried. My new wife had a daughter who became a mother at 16, for which she was not prepared. We took the little girl, Simone, and raised her as our own. Her mother took off. So it was just the three of us. We sent her to Catholic school and, again, life was pretty normal. She married and had a daughter and moved to Florida with her husband. We would visit once in a while, and then when we were in our late 70s, Simone suggested we move in with her. She had a beautiful large home with plenty of room, so we did, and it was nice to have a change of scene and get out of the cold winters.

"Simone belonged to a fellowship church, and my wife began attending with her. They asked me to come with them—they went twice a week—but I was raised Catholic and I didn't think I would fit into a Christian service that was based on the teachings of Jesus and the Bible, without all the rituals of an established religion. But they were so happy and raved about the people and the experience that I finally let them persuade me to join them one Sunday. That's when my life changed, at 80.

"I was warmly welcomed by members of the congregation, and within minutes I felt at home. The messages of love and acceptance, of hope and faith, were very encouraging; none of that fire and brimstone stuff. It was all joyous—a celebration—with Scripture reading and song. I guess you could call it more spiritual than religious, but whatever it was, I was captivated by it. I began attending Bible study, and, frankly, learned the Bible for the first time in my life."

Personal Courage—Rosie Ross

There is often a backstory to the lives of the centenarians in this book, as with active centenarians everywhere. They won't talk about it right away: they don't start out by saying, "I'm a cancer survivor," or "I had a triple bypass operation about 10 years ago." It's only after long conversations and getting to know them, that a behind-the-scenes look, usually in an offhand remark, reveals what they have gone through to make it to the century mark and beyond.

Like Rosie telling of the fire that left him with severe burns on his face, neck, hands, and arms when he was in his mid-90s.

He mentioned it casually one day, when we got to know him and spend time with him. He said something to the effect that he had had a kind of "facelift" from the skin grafts and surgeries after the fire, which had changed his appearance but left him with smoother skin. "My eyes are different," he pointed out, as we were going through his photos.

As we mentioned earlier, Rosie drove himself to his Friday night gigs at the supper club. Because it would be around 1:00 A.M. when he wrapped up and started the 40-minute drive back to his home in Prescott Valley, he decided to get a small camper and keep it at the edge of the parking lot near the woods so he could sleep overnight and drive home in the morning.

"One night I was wakened by the smell of fire. I used a kerosene stove for heat; it was near the door and somehow a fire started. The fire was small, but my first thought was just to get out of that tin box. I grabbed my horn and opened the door. That was a mistake. In an instant, the flames flared up like an explosion right in my face. I managed to stumble out and fortunately the owner was still there and called the medics.

"I spent several months at the VA hospital and had a lot of surgeries and skin grafts, and then rehab. Early on, the doctors told me I would never play the trumpet again because my lips were so badly burned. I told them I had to, so they kept working on me. I would lie there and practice the lip movements that make the sound on the horn. It hurt a lot, but I kept at it. Eventually, I got the mouthpiece from my horn and held it to my lips and would practice with that. This went on for months. The day I could put the mouthpiece back on the horn and make a sound come out was one of the happiest in my life."

RENEGOTIATING LIFE

Roberta McRaney

"They say lightning never strikes twice, but for me it did," Roberta McRaney, 101, begins. "The first time was in 1954, when our house burned to the ground. We rebuilt the house in the same spot. The second time was in the early 1970s. My husband and I were in Texas visiting our daughter and her family. A neighbor in Mississippi called to tell us our home in Lumberton had been hit by lightning. Again, it burned to the ground. This time was worse. In addition to everything else, I lost my family pictures. It was hard. But we rebuilt again.

"In the late 1970s we moved from Lumberton back to Mt. Olive. My husband's health was failing, and I wanted to be closer to family.

"I was born and raised near Mt. Olive, Mississippi. There were 10 of us kids. We grew up on a farm eating biscuits made of lard, bacon and eggs, and a lot of salt. In fact, they've been a part of my diet all my life. The only medicine I take is a pill for high blood pressure. My mother lived to 96 and many of my brothers and sisters into their 90s. For me, I think I worked all the fat off.

*"When I was a kid, I used to love to pick cotton and everyone laughed
at me, but I think all that bending and stooping has made me agile. I still am."*

"After my husband died, I lived by myself 'til I was 96. My daughter in Texas worried about me being alone. I wasn't worried a bit, but she wanted me to move to Texas to live with her and her family. I didn't want to move—I'd lived in Mississippi all my life. But I did. I don't like living in Texas, but I'm trying to make the best of it.

"I've stayed healthy and in good physical shape for all these years. I think it's because I love to work and still do. I especially like working outdoors. I never just sit around all day. These days I make myself useful around my daughter's house wherever I can. I sweep the driveway—it's quite long. I'm out there with my broom while the neighbors are using those blowers. It's quite a sight! Then I sweep the porch and the deck in back and pick up any fallen limbs in the yard. I really love any work outside. I do things around the house, too, like fold the laundry when it comes out of the dryer, and I always make my bed. I enjoy a fire in the fireplace and I keep it going by bringing in wood from the deck."

In January 2013, Roberta went back to Mississippi for a month-long visit with her other daughter, who still lives there. "I'm glad to be going home, even if just for little while," she says.

"I've learned to grieve about things and then let them go. You have to. I love people and life. I try to keep a positive attitude."

SPARKS OF THE SPIRIT

The centenarians who follow have a gleam in their eye, largely because they are doing things they like and that bring meaning and fulfillment to their lives.

"I am too blessed to be depressed," says Henry Carlton Smith, 100.

Helping Others—Living Well and Doing Good

Centenarians have a history of helping others and have learned that it makes them feel good. For many, it gives a sense of worth and self-esteem. It is gratifying when, at an advanced age, they can still have a positive effect on others' lives, they say.

"I look forward to the opportunity to help out younger generations," Gertrude Harradine, 100, said of participating in this book.

Gertrude "Trudy" Harradine, 100, grew up in Springfield, Massachusetts, in a French-Canadian enclave that included her grandparents, aunts, and uncles; 35 cousins and her five younger siblings—all of whom spoke only French. Her parents did not allow their children to speak English at home. "For the first five years of my life, I thought everyone spoke French," she says. "I had to learn English when I went to school."

When her father died at age 38, Trudy, then 14, went to work at a fruit and vegetable stand after school and on weekends, "to help my mother make ends meet." After high school she went to work at a local bank where she met her husband, Allen. "In those days, an unmarried woman at 27 was considered an old maid," she recalls. "It's just the way it was then. I continued working at another bank, married people were not allowed to work in the same bank, until my first son was born. Then I stayed home; it's what was expected for a woman to do.

"I was always very good with numbers and accounting. When we moved to Albion, New York, near Rochester, I helped my husband with his farm machinery business. After my husband died, my daughter Kaye wanted me to move to Michigan to live near her. But I loved my home and I didn't want to leave. I stayed on for 10 years there. Then, in my 80s, I sold it and moved to an apartment in a retirement center in Rochester. I stayed there for about 10 years—I wasn't ready to leave New York state yet. I really liked living there. Finally, in my 90s, I called Kaye and said, 'I'm ready,' so I moved to an apartment in a retirement center near her in Michigan."

A devout Catholic, Trudy believes it is her faith and a strong positive outlook on life that have gotten her to the century mark. "No one in my entire family lived especially long," she recalls. "I believe in the Serenity Prayer. Most people have heard it, but don't take the time to stop and think about its meaning. It has helped me throughout my life and every time I'm asked for my advice, this is what I tell people: 'God grant me the serenity to accept the things I cannot change; courage to change the things I can; and wisdom to know the difference.' I interpret this to mean that I must do my part as I live life, but believe that God will not let me fall down. I believe God has a plan for me, and that it is a good plan. I may not understand it, but I must trust in God and believe everything will turn out all right. I have people come back and thank me—it seems to help a lot of people.

"I use a walker now because my vision is failing, but I still go out for a two-mile walk every day when the weather cooperates. On others, I walk the hallways.

"I had a happy childhood and I wanted my children to have the same. I made it a point to always be home when they came from school."

Kaye is very proud of her mother. "She has a really wonderful attitude and I think that's what's kept her around so long. It's made a big impact on me."

Anna Orr, 102, is pleased to be doing well by staying active while doing things for others. "As the mother of 10 children, I always had to keep moving," she says. "Once alone, I took up power walking. I continue to walk every day, regardless of the weather, and once a week I walk a mile to the nursing home to help with the old folks who need it."

Often, the length of service of centenarians to their communities and participation in civic organizations goes on for decades. They were not in it for the short term and good volunteer work became an important part of many of their lives. Most centenarians, such as Jack Borden, exhibit a stick-to-itiveness that has contributed to the growth and well-being of their communities, and have been active members of charitable organizations for years. Others remain active in their university alumni associations and often serve on scholarship and fundraising boards.

*"I have been an active member of the Eastern Star for over 60 years
and am a member of the American Association of University
Women," says Kathryn Enix, 100.*

Andy Rasch, 107, says, "I've been helping others all my life, starting with my kid sister when we were teenagers. We were left orphans and put in a home. It was awful and we were abused, especially my sister. I was always a big kid so I could defend myself better. I promised her I would get her out of there as soon as I could, so I ran away when I was 15. I got a job and saved my money, and two years later I went back for her. She was in the yard and I stood by the iron fence—I know, it sounds like a movie scene, but it's true. At first she didn't recognize me, but I called to her and she came when she heard my voice. It's a long story and you don't want to hear the details, but I got her away from there and we lived together until she married at 21.

"I've continued to help other people whenever I could, ever since, especially veterans returning from wars, and those who are homeless. There is so much need in the world, everybody can do some good. It's been a big part of my life and I'm proud of it."

Identical twins Winnie Miller and Sally Lazarus, 100, share more than the background of a harsh childhood with Andy; they, too, have devoted a large part of their lives to doing good things for others, and it has, in part, defined them.

Growing up on the Lower East Side of New York City, the children of immigrant parents, they were sent to work at the age of 14 to help support their family. The girls attended high school at night, determined to get an education. In adulthood, they both took up causes to help those in need, even while rearing families of their own. They also shared the care of their sister who was stricken with multiple sclerosis.

*"We've never lived more than 20 minutes apart, for
most of our lives," Winnie said.*

Winnie Miller and Sally Lazarus

Sally started a program to create recordings of books for the blind long before this became a common service. Through her 80s she spent time at the local hospital with seniors who had no other visitors, and reading to children who were alone and scared, she said. Winnie worked with disabled children at a local home, and tutored disadvantaged youths for many decades. When her oldest son married a Swedish woman, Winnie learned to speak the language in her 60s so she could talk with her grandchildren. She made many trips to Sweden to visit them into her 90s. Now 100, Winnie is still traveling to California to visit her other grandchildren.

Lifelong learning and continued self-improvement was important to the twins. Winnie learned to play golf so she could join her husband, and learned to ski in her 50s to join her children on ski vacations. Sally learned to swim at 55 and to play tennis in her 60s. Both loved going to the theater and continued to do so into their late 80s; and Sally and her husband also took college courses at the nearby state university.

Winnie says, "Until our retirement years, before Sally and her husband moved to Florida, we did so many things together and were very close. But even then we talked by phone every day and we always celebrated all of the holidays together."

CENTENARIANS ON THE GO

"Whenever anyone says 'Go,' I'm ready," Kit Abrahamson, 105, exclaims.

Many centenarians we interviewed are not content just sitting around day after day. They still want to go out with friends and relatives, go to restaurants, go to the movies, and engage in other activities they have enjoyed earlier in their lives. They do not accept that they must stop doing these things just because they are old. As we have seen, centenarians are breaking the long-held stereotypes of life in later years.

Elsa Brehm Hoffmann: Come to the Cabaret

"I knew I had to remain active when I lost my husband. Bill was the love of my life and there could never be another man for me," Elsa Hoffmann says, expressing the viewpoint of many centenarian women who are widows, typically for two or more decades. "I've always enjoyed people. I like going out and being with others—having fun, socializing, and making new friends."

"I was the first single woman to be admitted to the country club
I wished to join. I think it's because I was a good golfer."

Elsa has remained a member and participates in all of the club's activities. Never wanting for an escort, she has a cadre of friends to accompany her to dances and other couples' events. Many are years younger, but with Elsa's spirited personality, the age difference doesn't matter.

"I enjoy getting dressed up and going out with people. We have a weekly luncheon at the club, a ladies group, after which we play pinochle. It's good mental stimulation, and of course we have plenty of time for 'girl talk.'" (Two of Elsa's good friends are also centenarians.) Elsa believes going out anywhere lifts the spirits. "Getting dressed as nicely as possible and mingling with others, even if it's at the grocery store, is important.

"It's no good sitting home alone all the time," she advises. "Sure, sometimes it's easier to just stay home, but after a while it becomes a habit and then it's even harder to go, and then the loneliness sets in and depression; it's just not healthy. So reach out to people—get out, even if you're alone. You will find your place, eventually. Just keep trying to make new friends. Our later years are no time to become a loner."

Mary Tysdal

The vivacious Mary Tysdal attributes her longevity to her strong faith, positive attitude, and resilience. "My husband of 65 years passed away when I was 98. He was

Mary Tysdal

100 and three months—isn't that amazing that we both made it to the century mark? For a lot of women, that would be a blow and perhaps they would seek the security of a retirement home. But that's not for me. I want to remain independent and live in my own home. So I adjusted and moved on. I mourned his loss, but you just can't dwell on it. I get along just fine here now. My kids were concerned that I would be isolated, since none of them live nearby. But I have a wonderful social network, and I'm sensible—I don't take risks. I have help come in when I need it, but otherwise I manage my home myself."

"Sure there are trials and tribulations, but on balance, just be glad to be alive. I know I am. I have a good family and friends, and I thank God he's let me stay here this long to be with them."

"My son and his wife came last year and surprised me with a 'do-over.' Lloyd and I had maintained our home, which we built in the '60s, but it needed updating and got it. It was fun. I chose the colors; my bedroom is lime green, my favorite, with flowered drapes and a fluffy down comforter. I have chocolate brown accent walls in the living room, my son's idea. It is truly my home now.

"When you're young, you don't think about getting old. But as Lloyd and I got on in years, we accepted it and had a good feeling about getting older and continuing to enjoy life. That was very rewarding. So many people are frightened. But you have to just get on with living and keep a good attitude and feel good about your own ability to cope. Resiliency is the main thing. If you can laugh at yourself, it's all OK. You need to have a sense of humor to get joy out of life.

"I'm getting along just fine and renewed my driver's license for another five years. I like going out for lunch with 'the girls,' all of whom are 20 years younger. I'm a Minnesota Twins fan, attend games occasionally, and travel often to visit my four children in California." Mary, now 103, continues her active schedule.

Ben Harris

When asked for the secret to his long life, Ben Harris, 100, replied: "I rode Harleys and chased young women." His wife, Mary, is 20 years his junior. Riding until he was 95, Ben claimed the title of oldest Harley rider east of the Mississippi. At 94, he rode to Dayton Beach for Bike Week. "I didn't feel a bit out of place," he says.

But that was not the longest trip for Ben in his 90s. At 92, he attended the 60th anniversary of the Allies' landing on the Palau Islands in the western Pacific, which is several hundred miles off the coast of the Philippines. The event was held at the Peleliu World War II Museum on Peleliu Island, location of one of the fiercest battles of World War II in 1944. Although he spent three and a half years as an artillery man, participating in invasions of numerous islands in the Pacific, including Guadalcanal, "I was never injured. But I figured my number was going to come up soon—I'd already lost two buddies from home. When the war ended I was in the Philippines on maneuvers practicing for the invasion of Japan. I was really glad that things were over."

Ben Harris

After the war, like many former servicemen, Ben used the GI Bill to train for a career, which in his case was to own a collision shop in California for 30 years. "I learned how to do body work and how to paint a car. It fit in well with my real love: Harleys. As we say, 'Live to ride, ride to live!'"

Joe Meyser

Joe Meyser, 105, was always an adventurous guy, with wanderlust. In the mid-1920s, he took up flying and was a barnstormer in the Midwest for a few years before earning his commercial pilot's license in 1929. He bought a three-seat plane and helped start a small airport in Iowa, were he flew freight and performed acrobatic barnstorming events with The Barry Circus on weekends. In the early 1930s, Joe moved to a larger airport in Illinois and was licensed to fly passengers. He flew until 1935, when he married and moved to Englewood, California. Joe's intention was to fly for North American Aviation, but he was hired instead in the engineering department and was involved in production of war planes for World War II.

The number of hours Joe flew in his early years qualified him for membership in the OX5 Club, founded in 1955 in Latrobe, Pennsylvania, following a rally of OX5 pilots. The OX5 engine, an early V-8 liquid-cooled aircraft engine built by Curtis, was the first U.S.-designed engine to enter mass production. Along with other aviation pioneers, Joe has enjoyed the camaraderie of other members now numbering 900, in different chapters across the nation. (Captain Grant is also a member on the East Coast). Nowadays, members no longer need to be pilots or mechanics.

Joe retired early in 1954. "You've got to have a job you enjoy," he believes. "I lived like that my whole life; I was lucky to have a wife who put up with it. In my 40s I realized that although I had a good job with a good career path, I knew it was not good for me—too stressful. So I got out and did what I wanted to do." Joe bought an orange grove and a health food store and ran it for five years; then bought an avocado grove and a Laundromat, which he ran until he was 70. "In the meantime, I'd bought a motor home and we traveled all over the West.

"When we moved to Champagne Village in Escondido, developed by Lawrence Welk who called it 'a little piece of heaven,' I took up golf. But I got a little restless, so at 72 I

Joe Meyser

bought land near Lake Tahoe and designed and built our house, doing a lot of the work myself. We lived in the Sierras for eight years. After my wife died when I was 80, I sold the home and traveled around in the motor home for a while, and then came back to Escondido. I bought another home next door to where we used to live. My wife and I had been friends with a couple on our block. I soon learned her husband had died in the meantime, so Doris and I became friends, and then she became my girlfriend. We lived five doors down from each other—it was a perfect arrangement, and we've been together ever since. I continued taking trips in the motor home and playing golf; I was getting pretty good.

"Doris and I made a lot of new friends, mostly women Doris knew. We'd go to the dinner dance every month and always sit at the same table with Doris's friends. To keep busy, I took up the hobby of silversmithing and traveled through the Southwest studying Indian jewelry, mostly Navaho. I designed and made necklaces, and gave them to my friends. Eventually, all of Doris's friends had necklaces and they would wear them to the dances. Our table became known as Joe's Harem."

At 90, Joe heard about the Senior Olympics and decided to enter, playing golf. He drove alone to the Huntsman World Senior Games in Utah, and won a medal in his age group. "I was hooked by the attention and went for the next six years. I got six gold medals." The following year, when he was 97, while driving to the games Joe was in the desert by himself when he developed a stomach problem that required hospitalization. "After that experience, I decided to give up the motor home, but I kept my license and kept driving until I was 100. I played golf until I was 103. Now I think I'm retired." But, he says, "the beat goes on."

A sizeable number of centenarians we have met have traveled internationally in their 80s and 90s, and a few, such as John Donnelly and Herbert Bauer, at 100 or close to it.

Betty Lucarelli said of her life with her second husband, "We traveled the world together, to Europe, South America, China, Japan, and local places in Florida and to Arizona."

A few, such as Betty, have developed a love for travel as they have grown older, for places near and far. Others have never outgrown it, and don't want to give it up.

James Hanson, 104, though, holds the record among our centenarians for having accumulated the most mileage as a traveler. "I've been all over the world," he says, "including Greenland and the South Pole."

KEEPING LIFE INTERESTING—COMMON INTERESTS, NOT COMMON AGE

Not everyone has the desire or the means to travel, but all centenarians enjoy the company of others, of all ages, and say that it enhances their life—whether they are interacting with friends and family or casual acquaintances.

As we have seen illustrated on these pages, socialization plays an important role in the lives of centenarians, just as it does at any other stage of life. Forging and maintaining connections to younger generations, whether it's with one generation or three, is essential to keeping life interesting, they say. "After all, there aren't many people around my own age, so I advise everyone as they grow older to make younger friends," says Garnett Beckman.

Often, the most readily available of younger generations can be found within one's family, especially grandchildren with whom many seem to share a special affection, and nieces and nephews who become as close as children as the years go on.

Addie Belle Roberts, 101, reports, "My granddaughter visits every week and we play cards or take a long walk in the garden. I can't walk as fast as I once could, and she never complains about my slow pace. We have a special connection and have for years. She is a great joy in my life."

Mary Pauline McNeil, 105, takes great satisfaction in knowing she is the ancestor to 29 great grandchildren. "I stay in touch with all of them."

Josephine Signorino, 100, spends time in the kitchen with her niece and grandniece when they come to visit, sharing her special recipes for stuffed artichokes and soups along with other dishes from her native Sicily. She loves to go shopping with them,

Josephine Signorino

but when it comes to household chores she is adamant about doing her housekeeping, shoveling snow, putting out the trash, and paying her own bills.

"I like to take care of myself, although I have 90 nieces and nephews who would be glad to help."

Dancing to Your Own Music—"Granpy" and Simone's Journey

"Eventually, I grew homesick and wanted to move back to Connecticut," Granpy said (see Religious/Spiritual Belief, earlier in this chapter). "So, on faith alone, Simone packed up and we drove north, not knowing where we would end up. But she said, 'Granpy,'everyone calls me that, 'you took me in when you had no idea what the future would hold for us, and I'll do that for you now. You will never be in a strange place. I'll take care of you, as you did for me.' My second wife had passed by this time. The degree of Simone's devotion to me is extraordinary; I am very grateful.

"We found an apartment in a senior living facility in Westport, and settled into a new life. It was hard for Simone, I know, although she's never complained. And then, neither of us had any idea I would live to 102! No one in my family had lived particularly long.

"Once here, we reached out to several of the churches to see if they would provide transportation for the other residents who did not have a way to get to church and they missed going, but got no help. So one day Simone said, 'Granpy, let's start our own Bible study right here.' At first we had difficulty getting the rec room for this use, but Simone called a lawyer in town and within the week we had permission to use the rec room on Sundays.

"'OK, what'll we do?' I asked Simone. She thought for a moment—we really hadn't planned this out—and she said, 'Well, we'll read the Bible and let people share their stories of faith, and sing.'

"'Sing?' I said, 'I can't sing!' So she got me to try it, with the songs we learned at the Christian church in Florida—not somber hymns actually, but joyous songs praising God and his presence in our lives.

"We put up a little notice on the bulletin board. Simone found a CD player and two microphones and some speakers, and I brought my Bible. We set up the room and waited.

"'Well, I might as well practice a song,' I said, and as I was singing *What a Friend We Have in Jesus*, one by one people began coming in. It was almost like I was calling them, except I know God was. To tell you the truth, I started to cry—I was overwhelmed with emotion. I just kept on singing other songs praising the Lord, and the folks kept coming in, some with walkers, some with canes, one in a wheelchair, pushing the heavy wheels herself, and some just fine and fit. Simone and I welcomed them, and I began reading from the Bible. Most had theirs with them, too. Then Simone passed the microphone and others read favorite passages, then we sang some more.

"In the following weeks, as people got comfortable being together, we would pass the microphone and people would share their stories or concerns, hopes, and fears. There was always a line for the microphone—seems everyone wanted to be able to talk and also to praise the Lord. It turned into our own little ministry, and we carried it on for a couple of years, and then someone else took it over to lead the group.

"Now, I watch religious programs on television often and have joined the 700 Club—I enjoy their fellowship and sense of community, and I get lots of material from them. I sing every day, praising the Lord for this beautiful world he has let me be a part of for so long. And, of course, prayer is a big part of my life. Simone and I begin each day with a prayer of thanks and end each day with one of gratitude. For me, it makes life complete."

Let the Good Times Roll

Rosie's story continues (see Personal Courage earlier in this chapter). About a year after the accident, and as soon as he was able, Rosie was back on stage at the supper club. He bought a larger trailer with a more secure heating system, but other than that his routine stayed the same. Each Saturday morning, he would get up early and drive home, where Doc, his roommate two years his junior, would have breakfast ready. They would sit at the small table in Rosie's kitchen—the dining room table had long ago been taken over by other items, including Rosie's pictures and memorabilia—and discuss the prior evening's events. Doc and his lady friend, Mary, were Friday night regulars. They would be among the first to arrive at the supper club and had a reserved table near the stage. After dinner and a couple of sets, they would drive home around 10:00.

"We are like 'The Odd Couple,'" Rosie says jovially of living with his roommate, Doc.

Asked how they came to be roommates, an arrangement they had enjoyed for several years, Rosie explains: "When Mary (Rosie's fifth wife—it took a while to find the right one, he says) and I moved here about 20 years ago, we had spent a couple of years at Lake Havasu before that, but it was too quiet for me there. I didn't like retirement, and I missed my friends here. Well, we bought this house, and the house was her domain, and I built on an addition, converting the two-car garage. I did most of the work myself (I used to be a carpenter as a day job years ago to support myself as a musician). I called it Rosie's Room, and put in a full-length wood bar, shelves, the whole nine yards, including a small dance floor and about 10 small tables and chairs. There are no windows except for a small one at the back behind the stage for some ventilation, and it had an entrance in the front separate from the house. There is a door between the two, of course—you have to go up a couple of steps to get into the house.

"Every Saturday night I would invite friends or they would just drop by for a drink and some music. We had an informal band, but really, anyone who loved music could come and play—we had an open microphone, so to speak. The bar was well stocked, but people were considerate and would bring a bottle sometimes to contribute. Mary would cook, and I have to give her credit because she hated the whole idea, she was a real homebody type. She made things for us like chili or finger food and set up a buffet table. She was a terrific cook. Then she'd leave and come back and check every once in a while if anything needed replenishing. She'd stay in the living room watching TV when she wasn't in the kitchen.

"I love a good party, and we had a great time. One of the regulars was a fellow everyone called 'Doc,' who had recently moved up to Prescott from Phoenix. He'd been a chiropractor—that's how he got his nickname. He'd lost his wife and didn't know anyone. My next-door neighbor, another Mary, and he became friends, and struck up a relationship. Doc lived quite a distance away, and my Mary and I would worry about him driving back alone late at night, and he wasn't the kind of guy who would stay next door, at least not then. So we invited him to spend Saturday nights with us, which worked out great. Mary would come over for brunch on Sunday and the four of us would have a good time. Eventually, Doc started staying Sunday nights, too. And then others, to the point where my wife suggested he just move in, informally, and stay whenever he wanted, which he did.

"It wasn't a burden because he and his Mary started traveling—they went everywhere—I've never seen anything like it! They went to the Far East, they went to Europe, and they took cruises. After my wife passed away, they drove one summer to Alaska and coaxed me into going along. I hated it, and flew back from Anchorage as soon as we got there. But they kept on going. Doc's planning his last big trip now.

"So we were both bachelors, and Doc sold his house and moved in permanently. That's when we became the Odd Couple. He makes sure I eat properly and take some of the vitamins that line the kitchen shelves. I have to do the dishes, though. He straightens up behind me when I leave a mess. Things like that. But we get along fine. Doc likes the parties. I keep things hoppin'. Doc reached the century mark, too. That had been his goal all along."

CONTEMPORARY CENTENARIANS—THINKING AND FEELING YOUNG

Not feeling their chronological age is a common thread among most centenarians we interviewed. They say they feel on average at least 20 years younger, which would be around 80. When asked at what age they think people are considered to be in old age, they'll say in one's 90s. "There may be old people out there," as one centenarian said, "But I'm not one of them."

"I don't know what age I feel like, but it's certainly not 100."
RUTH PROSKAUER SMITH, 102

With active centenarians, this is a familiar refrain. "I never think about age," Gertrude Knowlton says. "I think about what I want to do each day. My theory is age is an attitude. I've never paid attention to age. I've always been younger than my biological age."

"Over the past 20 years I've felt 15 to 20 years younger
than my chronological age."
MARY FLEMING, 103

While there is a sense of pragmatism about their limits, centenarians are young at heart. Active centenarians do not live in the past, although they honor it as part of their life experience. They are interested in contemporary life and in the world around them.

"Be comfortable with your life," Janet Brooks, 100, advises, "throughout all its
seasons." Or, as Dorothy Oellers, 100, says, "Bloom where you are planted."

Helping others, having realistic expectations, forgiving those who have wronged us, keeping a positive attitude, and being grateful for what one has, seem essential; and most say they are satisfied with their lives and wouldn't change a thing. This is a common theme among centenarians: "I'm enjoying every day of my life." To be able to say that at the pinnacle of advanced age is about as good as life gets.

Charles Kayhart—Communications Pro

Take Charles Kayhart, 101, for example. On the one hand he takes pride in staying active, and like many centenarians could pass for 80. He enjoys learning and keeping pace with new technology. "I spent a large part of my life in the technology aspects of the communications industry, and it's something I've always been interested in. I correspond by e-mail all the time—no more snail mail. I'm fascinated to see where technology is going, and I want to remain a part of it.

"For my birthday, I just bought myself an iPad, and it's really cool.
And whatever comes next, I'm going to have one of those, too."

On the other hand, he doesn't forget important things from his past. As a veteran, Charles enjoyed taking a trip to Washington, D.C., to tour the World War II Memorial. It gave him a chance to revisit his past. "I went as part of the Honor Flight organization. I was the oldest participant in the group. It was great meeting and talking to other veterans and honoring those who didn't make it home. I was on Iwo Jima at the height of the battle.

"When it was my time to get into the war—after college and working several years as an engineer in the growing radio and electronic field, an area I've liked since I was a kid—I joined the Army Signal Corps. They sent me to Harvard and MIT to study radar and assigned me to the Army Air Corp. I was stationed briefly at Robbins Field in Georgia before being sent to Hawaii and then Iwo Jima.

"We landed two days after the flag had been raised on Mt. Suribachi," Charles continues. "I was commanding an Army Signal Corp battalion. Our job was to establish a communications system so that all the units on the island could be coordinated. After six months, I was ordered back to headquarters in Hawaii.

"While waiting for my air transport to return, I saw what I now know was
the Enola Gay flying overhead to Hiroshima to drop the atomic bomb."

"I became the commanding officer of the inter-island radio station in Hawaii, and stayed on for a while after the war ended. In 1946 I left the military as a Captain and returned to civilian life. Continuing my career on the engineering side of the communications industry, I joined Magnavox in 1947 as their first field engineer, and eventually retired in 1976 in Greenville, Tennessee, after founding a new division for the company. I decided then that this would be my home for the rest of my life."

Besides keeping very current on new technology, Charles continues to drive and mows his own lawn with a push mower. "Life is great fun," says Charles, and you can tell that the moment you speak with him.

Charles "Cliff" Kayhart

Astrid Thoenig—Today's Modern Woman

For Astrid Thoenig, 103, staying current with the times is a requirement. "I'm still working full time, and I love it." Over her long life Astrid has had many roles along with dedicated career woman: wife, mother, community volunteer, single working Mom, entrepreneur, remarriage, third career, caring daughter to her mother, and involved grandmother. "I'm blessed," she believes.

"When people hear me on the phone or watch me do my work,
they mistake me for someone 40 years younger."

"I'm not quick to tell my chronological age. It's not that I have any tricks or secrets to staying younger—this is just the way I am and always have been."

Astrid is a fair-minded, practical, no-nonsense woman, with an engaging personality—and she can tell a good story.

"My parents were Swedish immigrants," she begins. "My father and a sister died in the 1918 flu pandemic, when I was nine. My mother and another sister were both sickened, but I never got sick at all. My mother remarried, and my stepfather was very good to us. I always called him Dad.

"In high school I learned to sew and do needlework, skills that I used to make most of my clothing throughout my life. I also learned typing and stenography and other business skills that would provide the foundation for a career. Early on, I dreamed of having a career. After graduation, most girls looked forward to marriage and a family, but I was eager to go to work. So eager, in fact, that during Christmas recess in my senior year I worked at a local bank. I loved working and thought I would stay on at the bank rather than finish out my senior year. My mother was so wise; instead of telling me I couldn't do that, she went to the bank president and asked him not to offer me a job until I had graduated. I didn't find out until years later. At the time I was disappointed, but by the time I'd graduated in June 1928, I had decided I wanted to work for a lawyer and set about finding a job with a local law firm. If there had been paralegal positions at that time, I would have followed that course.

"As it was, I worked for a couple of local lawyers for the next three years, enjoying the challenging and interesting work. Then I wanted a change, so I took a job on Wall Street in Manhattan at an import-export business. I thought I would be an old maid, and I was OK with that, except I began to wish for a family of my own. On vacation at Lake George one summer with my mother and my sister, a couple of boys came over to us as we were sitting by the water. We talked and discovered they were from New Jersey also. We exchanged phone numbers. The boys offered to leave the canoe they had rented with us to use since they had paid for it and were leaving before the rental was up. We accepted and enjoyed paddling around the lake. When we returned it, we discovered we had been stuck with the bill—it had not been paid in advance. It was an innocent mistake, but Stewart was so embarrassed when I told him when he called—I teased him about it—it was a riot. We began dating and were married in 1937. I continued working and he was a manager at *Collier's* magazine. Even though it was during the Depression, we were all right. For many others, though, it was awful.

"In 1942, with the birth of our son, John, I became a stay-at-home mom. I was contented. Then my life suddenly changed. My husband was drafted when John was only 18 months old. They hadn't been taking fathers until then, but suddenly there was a shortage of men, and he was called up and sent to France. A few weeks later, that practice was stopped, and others didn't have to serve, my brother-in-law for one. It just shows how arbitrary life can be—my husband missed it by four weeks. He was wounded in battle and earned the Purple Heart for his bravery. But his injuries left him totally disabled to do any physical work, so he was given a desk job in Atlanta, where he served out the rest of the war. He never really recovered from his injuries and died when John was nine, the same age as I was when I lost my father.

"In order to support us and still be home with John, I started working from home doing typing for lawyers and other professionals in the area, and even a judge. It was an unusual arrangement in those days. But my friend's husband was a lawyer and he lost his secretary, so he began coming over in the evenings and giving me dictation and I would type it up and deliver it to his office the following day. My home business grew by word of mouth. I was a good typist and stenographer, and I enjoyed the work. If you enjoy what you're doing, you do it well. After six years, I was so busy that I was about to hire a girl to work with me and start a formal business. Then, on my mother's birthday, we were at a restaurant celebrating. My dad was a home builder. One of the patrons recognized him and came over to the table. I was introduced to Ray Thoenig, an architect who worked for my dad. One thing led to another and we married.

Astrid Thoenig

"The only problem was, Ray was vehemently opposed to having a working wife—even working at home. And so I gave up my business and settled into being a housewife. I kept busy volunteering in the community—activities my husband approved of— with organizations such as the Red Cross and United Way. Then I was asked to volunteer part time for the borough treasurer's office. I really liked that because it was interesting and substantive. It soon led to the offer of a full-time job, so I said to Ray, 'I'm so bored, I just can't stay home any longer. I'll do all the things I should around the house and as your wife, but I've just got to go back to work.' Over his objection, I took the job of assistant treasurer, but when I was offered the treasurer's job, Ray put his foot down and said no. He didn't want me traveling and attending meetings at night as I would have had to do, so I stayed in the assistant treasurer's job. He was earning a good living for us as an architect, and in the 1950s and early 1960s, for our generation it was considered a negative for a man whose wife worked outside the home. It was seen as though he couldn't support her. It was all nonsense, of course, but that's the way it was. It was a status symbol for a woman to be a full-time stay-at-home wife—at least for the man.

"I regret not taking the job. After 16 years of marriage, I was widowed again. But now I had a chance of a lifetime. When my son, John, came to me with the idea of starting an insurance business, I jumped at the chance. I was 68. I quit my job and we went into business together. Third time's a charm, they say. I've worked full time at the business as secretary, office manager—handling all the finances and bills—and keeping everything in order and on track since then. It's a joy to be doing work I love alongside the people I love. My grandson has joined the business. But when I walk through that door, it's all business and our relationship ends until the end of the day. I'm treated like any other employee—no favoritism or nepotism. If I want time off, I ask for it. That way, other employees respect me, because I'm one of them and there's never any tension in the office that I'm getting special treatment.

"I'm using the computer in addition to the fundamental skills I learned decades ago; it's a nice mix. I love to work, and I love the work I do."

"It must be terribly unpleasant, even difficult, for people who don't like their jobs. Most of all, I love to type. It's like playing the piano, and I make very few mistakes. With a computer you're using your brain and your typing skills, and it's a good way to keep your mind sharp and maintain your coordination. But I still like the sound of a typewriter. I don't miss carbon copies, though—that was a nightmare if you made a mistake, having to erase it on every page.

"Except for a botched hip operation when I was 98, the result of a slip, my health has always been good. I had to give up driving then and that was hard, and I'm slower now. I was always very quick—I hate being slowed down. But at least I'm not in a wheelchair. I live alone in my own apartment and spend the evenings reading and knitting. I love to knit, I always have. Right now, I'm working on an afghan with a very intricate pattern. I don't like to do easy patterns. They're boring. I like the challenge. And I think to myself, 'I want to stay around to finish this afghan,' and then I'll start a sweater and want to be around to finish the sweater. I'm a fatalist, I suppose. I think when it's your time, you leave. Until then, I intend to enjoy my life just the way it is."

On a personal note, Astrid shares advice to those who have elders in their lives. "It's important to keep occupied even when you're older, and it's important for people to have a sense of satisfaction. Others can help them achieve this with a little ingenuity." She tells of her mother, who lived to be 101. "She had been a hardworking woman all her life, and she was an avid knitter. For years and years she knitted beautiful baby garments—sweaters, booties, hats—they were her specialty, and she would donate them to the church or to charities to sell at fundraisers and to organizations that helped people in need. When she began to lose her vision because of macular degeneration, she chose to live in a group home. She didn't want to be a burden on me because I was working and she didn't want me to quit and take care of her. She continued her knitting and would offer her items for sale to benefit the home. As her sight diminished, she could no longer see when she dropped a stitch, ruining the item. I made an arrangement with the woman who ran the home that I would supply the yarn and she would continue to display my mother's baby clothes as though they were for sale, and change them out periodically. We kept that arrangement until the end of my mother's life, and she was so pleased of the baby clothes she was able to make to help others.

"There are small things we can do to help give our elders a sense of dignity and of remaining who they are," she believes.

Of course, that's for people when they grow old—and Astrid is not there yet! She'll be the first to tell you.

Irving Kahn, Money Manager

We met Irving Kahn, then 104, at his Wall Street money management firm, Kahn Brothers. He made it clear that he was not interested in being recognized because of his age, but rather because of his work. "I don't see what all the fuss is about over being a centenarian," he said. "I'd rather be thought of because of what we do—successfully managing people's money." Mr. Kahn is chairman and one of his sons is president of the firm. However, he did concede that he enjoyed kicking off his 100th birthday by ringing the opening bell at the New York Stock Exchange. At lunch recently in his office, Mr. Kahn, now 107, said he was still actively involved in managing investments for his clients.

As a student at Columbia University, he was a teaching assistant to Ben Graham, whose Value Investment philosophy he learned and has since followed throughout his career. He worked with Professor Graham on statistical material for Graham's major work, *Security Analysis* (co-authored with David Dodd), published in 1934. "This book is still in print, and is widely regarded as the 'bible' of investment philosophy.

We remained friends for 30 years, and in fact I met my wife, Ruth, at one of Professor Graham's lectures."

Mr. Kahn tells an anecdote from his long career. "I made my first trade, a short sale of $300 of stock two days before the crash, and I doubled my money and watched those around me lose their shirts as things fell apart. Even as an inexperienced kid just starting out, I could see that there was a lot of gambling on borrowed money, and it would never last."

Mr. Kahn's career encompassed associations with such well-known firms as Loeb Rhodes and Lehman Brothers, before founding Kahn Brothers in 1978 with his two sons. He was one of the first persons to take the examination to become a Certified Financial Analyst in 1963.

CATCH THE SPIRIT: FORGET AGING GRACEFULLY— AGE EXCELLENTLY!

This general feeling among centenarians of being decades younger than indicated by their birth certificates is good news for Baby Boomers and the generations just ahead of them. Given the role models we have seen in this book, the ubiquitous precept to "age gracefully" is outmoded. Contemporary centenarians, who say they are enjoying life at the pinnacle of age, show that it is possible to instead "age excellently."

"I love my life and I enjoy each day," says Inez Houston, 100.

And Boomers, who have gone far beyond the normal societal limits and expectations since the mid-1960s, have the opportunity now to set this standard, to create a "cool old age," if they choose, and in doing so to leave an example for younger generations to follow. In the process, the Boomer generation will produce an abundance of octogenarians, nonagenarians, and centenarians.

Boomers have the ability and the opportunity to emulate the active centenarian model, thus creating a better standard of living as we age, as a cultural norm. To paraphrase Dylan Thomas's admonition, Boomers and new centenarians, like today's active centenarians, "will not go gentle into that good night." Striving to live life to the fullest is an attractive alternative to the societal cliché "aging gracefully" or just "running out the clock." This cultural norm is passive and passé in the twenty-first century. It is time for a new alternative for life in later years. This is a paradigm shift that encapsulates what we see in the lives of centenarians in this book. The term *aging excellently* is a concept that is personalized and individualized.

In this, active centenarians are our role models. They show us in this book how they have persevered through life's challenges. For them it was the Great Depression, World War II, illnesses that would be easy to cure today, the loss of loved ones, and many other of life's vicissitudes. They show us the importance of making financial soundness a priority, caring for their health, taking satisfaction from their life's work, and finding new activities after retirement. It's a desire to continue to contribute to their families and communities in whatever way they can, if only by being a good example and keeper of the zeitgeist (i.e., the family lore).

"Power" of Centenarians

And then there are some centenarians who are endowed with "special powers," at least in the eyes of their descendants—Sidney Kronish, for one.

Sidney Kronish, PhD, has enough credentials of his own, which include Navy veteran, tenured economics professor (retired), author, and labor mediator. "My first book was published in 1955 and my latest in 1995," he says. "I am a consummate reader. I read the *New York Times* cover to cover every day and several books a month. I enjoy discussing current affairs with anyone who will listen, particularly with those who hold opposing views on politics." Adding to his luster was an interview on CBS National News a few months before his 100th birthday in June 2012.

But it's his role as patriarch of the family that garners the most attention, at least from his great great great nephew, Ben, age four, who, upon hearing that his great great

Sidney Kronish

great Uncle Sidney had turned 100, was so intrigued that he frequently made observations such as:

"Hey Mommy, did you know that great great great Uncle Sidney is the tallest person in the whole world, because he is 100.

Hey Mommy, did you know that great great great Uncle Sidney is the strongest man ever, because he is 100.

Hey Mommy, did you know that great great great Uncle Sidney is the fastest person ever, because he is 100.

Hey Mommy, did you know that great great great Uncle Sidney is the bravest person in the whole wide world, because he is 100.

(And the family favorite)

Hey Mommy, did you know that great great great Uncle Sidney can stick his head in outer space! (Wow Ben, I didn't know that!) Yeah, because he is 100."

Undoubtedly, there will be new amazing adventures of great great great Uncle Sidney revealed.

For every party the family has or goes to, Ben asks if his great great great Uncle Sidney has been invited.

A FORMULA FOR LONGEVITY

Longevity = Genes + Lifestyle + Attitude + Wisdom + Innovations

It would be wonderful to have a formula to live to be 100, however, nothing can guarantee longevity. Still, this book shows how many of our centenarians have used their wisdom and rapidly moving technological and medical innovation to add extra years to their lives. Of course, having the right genes is a major factor, and modern research is working to unlock these longevity keys. This work shows great promise to extend all of our lives.

A TOAST TO FUTURE CENTENARIANS

It is a great distinction to live to celebrate 100 years and beyond. We have learned from this book the attributes and lifestyles of many centenarians who have mastered how to live long and live well. These qualities, shared by our centenarians in differing individual degrees, form the Centenarian Spirit that is so vital to aging excellently. You do not have to be a centenarian to capture, keep, and enjoy the Centenarian Spirit. We can make the most of our lives by integrating some of their attitudes, behaviors, and wisdom into our daily routines at business and at home. Nothing is a better teacher than experience, and our centenarians have freely shared theirs with us.

We hope you will benefit from what these inspirational centenarians have passed along, and that it will contribute to creating a better, more fulfilling life.

Recalling Ponce de Leon's quest, we can't help but think that happening upon our centenarians, he surely would have proclaimed he found the proverbial Fountain of Youth.

APPENDIX

Sharing the Wisdom

CENTENARIANS ARE A VERY SPECIAL SEGMENT OF OUR POPULATION, and we have captured much of their vast knowledge, wisdom, wit, and advice to share with you in *Celebrate 100*. But virtual gold mines of stories and "secrets" abound among seniors marching toward the century mark.

In your world of relationships, there are older people who have stories to tell—wise, witty, funny, sad, practical, and off-the-wall. They can be captured and shared with our younger generation. You have a diverse universe to choose from: family members, friends, neighbors, colleagues, teachers, or coaches—people who are one or two generations ahead of you on the pathway of life.

We encourage you to use a video camera, contact the person, and ask if you may visit them to ask their advice about some questions relating to life, money, and work. Tell them how valuable and meaningful it will be to you and many others to capture their stories and share them with family and friends. Be sure and take your camera for photos.

In this appendix we have provided 100 sample questions that you may choose from to get the communication flowing and provide some natural direction from family heritage through childhood, adult, golden, and platinum years. And come up with your own unique questions that will help the stories and "secrets" to flow.

Please do it now while *Celebrate 100* is fresh in your heart and on your mind.

100 QUESTIONS TO CAPTURE THE SECRETS TO A LONG AND FULFILLING LIFE

Family Heritage

1. Where were you born?
2. What is your date of birth?
3. What do you know about your family's genealogy?
4. What is your family's ethnic background?
5. What language(s) were spoken in your home?
6. Do you have any interesting or famous relatives in your family tree?
7. When did your first family member come to America? Where did they settle?
8. What do you remember about your grandparents? How did they meet?
9. Where were your parents born? What was their courtship like?
10. What did your grandparents and parents do for a living?
11. Share a funny story or special memory about your grandparents or parents.
12. Describe your mother's best qualities.
13. Describe your father's best qualities.
14. Did you have any brothers and sisters? Names? Birth order? Age spread?
15. How long did your siblings live, or how old are they now?

Childhood Years

16. What is your earliest childhood memory?
17. What was your best friend's name?
18. Tell me about your siblings. Who were you closest to?
19. What did you do for fun in each season of the year?
20. What kinds of toys did you play with?

21. What kinds of activities did you participate in?
22. What sports did you play?
23. Describe your first school. Favorite subject? Favorite teacher?
24. How did your family celebrate birthdays and holidays?
25. What was your favorite holiday?
26. Did you have any pets or raise farm animals?
27. What's your funniest pet story?
28. Where was your favorite place to visit as a child?
29. What was your most memorable vacation?
30. Where did your family go to get food and clothing?
31. How did you travel from place to place?
32. What was your first chore or job? Do you remember how much you got paid?
33. Who first taught you about work, money, and life? What were the core lessons?
34. How would you describe yourself as a child?
35. Tell me about the first time you saw a train, plane, or automobile. Were you a passenger?
36. What event, personal or historical, left the greatest impression on you as a child?
37. What role did God play in your family's life when you were growing up? Did you attend church or synagogue?

Adulthood Years

38. How old were you when you first married? Describe your courtship.
39. Tell about your wedding and honeymoon.
40. Did you have children? Tell me about each one.
41. Did you or your spouse serve in the military? In World War II? What branch of service?

42. What level of education have you completed? Where?
43. At what age did you first start working to earn a living?
44. What was your occupation? Spouse's occupation?
45. What was the average number of hours you worked per week?
46. Did you enjoy your work? Did you view work as a burden or a blessing? Why?
47. What do you remember about the "Roaring Twenties"?
48. What do you remember about the Great Depression? How did it affect you/change your worldview?
49. When did you buy your first car? Home? Describe them. How did you pay for them?
50. What did you do with your money? Percentage saved? Invested? Donated to charity?
51. If you were given a million dollars today, what would you do with it?
52. Who most influenced your values, career path, and life choices? (Mom, Dad, grandparent, teacher, boss, mentor)
53. What event, personal or historical, left the greatest impression on you as an adult?
54. What role did God play in your life during your working/parenting years?

Golden Years

55. What age were you when you retired?
56. If you could live life over again, would you pursue a different type of work?
57. What was your greatest success at work? In life?
58. What was the most fun thing you ever did?
59. Have you ever smoked? If yes, at what age did you quit?
60. How has your health been throughout your life? Any major illnesses?
61. In your lifetime, have you been on special diets or exercise programs to stay healthy?

62. What advice do you have for younger people about work?

63. What advice do you have for younger people about health?

64. What advice do you have for younger people about money?

65. What advice do you have for younger people about marriage?

66. What advice do you have for younger people about parenting?

67. What advice do you have for younger people about life in general?

68. Do you feel your chronological age? If not, what age do you feel?

69. Do you still drive a car? If not, at what age did you stop driving?

70. Have you experienced a lot of stress during your life?

71. Which season of your life have you enjoyed most? Why?

72. How did the events of 9/11/2001 affect you?

73. Would you like to live to be 100? Why or why not?

Platinum Centenarian Years

74. Did you ever think you would live to be 100?

75. What's the greatest thing about being your age?

76. What's your secret for living to your age?

77. Do you still vote?

78. Who was your favorite U.S. president? Why?

79. If you could give one piece of advice to the current president, what would it be?

80. Who did you admire the most in your lifetime?

81. Who influenced your character most?

82. What role does God, religion, or spirituality play in your life today?

83. What activities do you most enjoy today?

84. Do you: read, watch TV, cook, play music, etc.?

85. What types of books, TV shows, food, and music do you enjoy most?

86. Do you use any of the following: cell phone, Internet, voice mail, iPod, computer, e-mail, DVDs, or CDs?

87. Of all the inventions during your lifetime, which one(s) changed your life the most?

88. What has been the key to your happiness?

89. What do you consider to be your greatest success in your life?

90. Do you have any regrets?

91. Are there any opportunities that passed you by or dreams you didn't pursue?

92. How do you define the word *rich?*

93. What wisdom and advice would you give to the younger generation today about education?

94. What wisdom and advice would you give to the younger generation today about marriage?

95. What wisdom and advice would you give to the younger generation today about work?

96. What wisdom and advice would you give to the younger generation about money?

97. What wisdom and advice would you give to the younger generation today about debt?

98. What wisdom and advice would you give to the younger generation today about saving?

99. What wisdom and advice would you give to the younger generation today about health?

100. How would you like others to remember you?

NOTES AND FURTHER READING

AUTHOR INTERNET CONNECTIONS

Authentic Wisdom from America's Centenarians, Steve Franklin, Ph.D.
www.100wisdom.com

> Our mission is to capture the wisdom of America's centenarians and share it
> with the younger generation.

National Centenarian Awareness Project, Lynn Peters Adler, J.D.
www.adlercentenarians.org

> Inspiring Positive Aging. Our nonprofit organization celebrates active centenarians
> as role models for the future of aging. On our blog, we discuss the lifestyles of active
> centenarians and what it's like to live to 100 and beyond.

SUGGESTED READING LIST

Adler, Lynn Peters. *Centenarians: The Bonus Years*. Sante Fe, New Mexico: Health
  Press, 1995.
Bortz, II, Walter M. and Randall Stickrod. *The Roadmap to 100: The Breakthrough
  Science of Living a Long and Healthy Life*. New York: Palgrave MacMillian, 2010.
Buettner, Dan. *The Blue Zones: Lessons for Living Longer from the People Who've Lived
  the Longest*. Washington, D. C., National Geographic Press. 2008.

————. *Blue Zones: 9 Secrets to Live a Long Life.* Washington, D. C., National Geographic Press, 2012.

Butler, Robert N. *The Longevity Prescription: The 8 Proven Keys to a Long, Healthy Life.* New York: Penguin Group, 2010.

Friedman, Howard S. and Leslie R Martin. *The Longevity Project: Surprising Discoveries for Health and Long Life from the Landmark Eight-Decade Study.* New York: Hudson Street Press, 2011.

Goldberg, Elkhonon. *The Wisdom Paradox: How Your Mind Can Grow Stronger As Your Brain Grows Older.* New York: Penguin, 2006.

Gupta, Sanjay. *Chasing Life.* New York: Hachette Book Group U.S.A., 2007.

Nuland, M.D., Sherwin B. *The Art of Aging: A Doctor's Prescription for Well Being.* New York: Random House, 2007.

Pillemer, Karl. *30 Lessons for Living: Tried and True Advice for the Wisest Americans.* New York: Penguin, 2012.

Perls, Thomas T. and Margery Hutter Silver, with John F. Lauerman. *Living to 100: Lessons in Living to Your Maximum Potential at Any Age.* New York: Perseus Book Group, 1999.

Robbins, John. *Healthy to 100.* New York: Ballantine Books, 2007.

CENTENARIAN RESEARCH STUDIES

Georgia Centenarian Study, ran from 1988 through 2009 under the direction of Leonard Poon, Ph.D., at the University of Georgia Institute of Gerontology. www.publichealth.uga.edu/geron/research/centenarian-study.

New England Centenarian Study, begun in 1994, Thomas Perls, M.D., director, University of Boston. www.bumc.bu.edu/centenarian.

Gerontology Research Group, founded in 1990 by Stephen Coles, M.D., Ph.D., UCLA,. Focus is on supercentenarians, people age 110 and older. www.grg.org.

The Longevity Genes Project, began in 2002 , Dr. Nir Barzilai, Director, Albert Einstein College of Medicine, www.einstein.yu.edu/centers/aging/longevity-genes-project.

PHOTO CREDITS

Ron Gilbert, courtesy Lifetouch Portrait Studio.

George Blevins, National Senior Games Association.

Trudi Fletcher, photo by Ellen Sussman, courtesy of Green Valley News, Green Valley, AZ.

Margaret Dunning, photo by Neil Rashba, courtesy of Rashba.com.

Thanks to the families of the centenarians in this book who provided some of the photos.

ABOUT THE AUTHORS

STEVE FRANKLIN, PHD

Steve Franklin is an author, educator, speaker, businessman, and centenarian wannabe. He is passionate about capturing the wisdom, wit, and advice of centenarians across America and energetically sharing it with the younger generation.

He co-authored two major business textbooks that were adopted in hundreds of colleges and universities across America, educating thousands of college students about principles of business success. His articles were published in over 40 publications, and his research was reported in numerous periodicals throughout the nation including The Christian Science Monitor, Los Angeles Times, Atlanta Journal Constitution, Dallas Morning News, Chicago Tribune, and many more. He has appeared on dozens of radio and television programs, including the Gannett Broadcasting "Million Dollar Dreams" series aired throughout the country and watched by millions of viewers.

Dr. Franklin was a tenured professor and associate dean, and received the number one teaching evaluation by students three times at Emory University's Goizueta Business School. He has consulted with and delivered hundreds of keynote speeches to major organizations throughout North America, Europe, South Africa, and Dubai including Coca-Cola, General Electric, Federal Express, Northwestern Mutual, UPS, AT&T, Johnson and Johnson, IBM, Chick-fil-A. While at Emory, he cofounded the Emory Center for Healthcare Leadership and now serves on the Board of Regents at Oxford University's Harris Manchester College in England and is the Chairman of the Board of Governors for The American University in Dubai.

For the past several years he has visited, videotaped, interviewed, dined, danced, laughed a lot, cried a little, and even exercised with centenarians all across America to capture and share their secrets and love for long and abundant life. Steve's goal is to live 120 years healthy, wealthy, and wise with his incredible wife, Elaine. He is over halfway there! His web site is: www.100wisdom.com.

LYNN PETERS ADLER, JD

Lynn Peters Adler is founder and director of the nonprofit National Centenarian Awareness Project, and is an expert on the lifestyles of active centenarians. For over 28 years, Lynn has been an advocate of positive aging. She has focused a spotlight on the lives of active centenarians as role models for the future of aging, replacing negative stereotypes with positive views of what is possible in our later years. The breath and depth of her experience with centenarians and their families spans an entire generation, giving her a unique perspective as reflected in her work and in *Celebrate 100*. Lynn conducted the first nationwide survey of centenarian lifestyles and is the author of the award-winning book *Centenarians: The Bonus Years*. She co-produced the first centenarian documentary, *Centenarians Tell It Like It Is*, which aired on PBS, and authored an inspirational calendar, *Age with Grace: The Centenarian Spirit*, published by Cedco Publishing.

Lynn has been featured in major media, including a CNN special, *Newsweek* and *People* magazines, the *New York Times* and the *Wall Street Journal*, and numerous local and regional media formats. She has appeared on all national television networks as well as various cable stations and radio programs. In 2008 she assisted the production and appeared in a Barbara Walters Special "Living to 150: Can You Do It?," with four of her centenarian friends.

She was a two-term member of the Governor's Advisory Council on Aging in Arizona, past chairman of the Phoenix Mayor's Aging Services Commission, and member of the Arizona Attorney General's Task Force on Elder Abuse. She founded Arizona's Centenarian Program in 1985–1986, and was instrumental in helping other states and entities establish similar programs.

Lynn is a graduate of Sarah Lawrence College and holds a law degree. She now lives in Fairfield County, Connecticut, and is a writer, speaker, and consultant.

Her web site, www.adlercentenarians.org, includes the blog *Live to 100 and Beyond* and is the home of the National Centenarian Awareness Project. All proceeds she receives from the sale of *Celebrate 100* will go to furthering the work of NCAP.